The Poetry of Algernon Charles Swinburne

VOLUME X – TRISTRAM OF LYONESSE

Algernon Charles Swinburne was born on April 5th, 1837, in London, into a wealthy Northumbrian family. He was educated at Eton and at Balliol College, Oxford, but did not complete a degree.

In 1860 Swinburne published two verse dramas but achieved his first literary success in 1865 with Atalanta in Calydon, written in the form of classical Greek tragedy. The following year "Poems and Ballads" brought him instant notoriety. He was now identified with "indecent" themes and the precept of art for art's sake.

Although he produced much after this success in general his popularity and critical reputation declined. The most important qualities of Swinburne's work are an intense lyricism, his intricately extended and evocative imagery, metrical virtuosity, rich use of assonance and alliteration, and bold, complex rhythms.

Swinburne's physical appearance was small, frail, and plagued by several other oddities of physique and temperament. Throughout the 1860s and 1870s he drank excessively and was prone to accidents that often left him bruised, bloody, or unconscious. Until his forties he suffered intermittent physical collapses that necessitated removal to his parents' home while he recovered.

Throughout his career Swinburne also published literary criticism of great worth. His deep knowledge of world literatures contributed to a critical style rich in quotation, allusion, and comparison. He is particularly noted for discerning studies of Elizabethan dramatists and of many English and French poets and novelists. As well he was a noted essayist and wrote two novels.

In 1879, Swinburne's friend and literary agent, Theodore Watts-Dunton, intervened during a time when Swinburne was dangerously ill. Watts-Dunton isolated Swinburne at a suburban home in Putney and gradually weaned him from alcohol, former companions and many other habits as well.

Much of his poetry in this period may be inferior but some individual poems are exceptional; "By the North Sea," "Evening on the Broads," "A Nympholept," "The Lake of Gaube," and "Neap-Tide."

Swinburne lived another thirty years with Watts-Dunton. He denied Swinburne's friends access to him, controlled the poet's money, and restricted his activities. It is often quoted that 'he saved the man but killed the poet'.

Swinburne died on April 10th, 1909 at the age of seventy-two.

TO MY BEST FRIEND
THEODORE WATTS

I DEDICATE IN THIS BOOK

Spring speaks again, and all our woods are stirred,
And all our wide glad wastes aflower around,
That twice have heard keen April's clarion sound
Since here we first together saw and heard
Spring's light reverberate and reiterate word
Shine forth and speak in season. Life stands crowned
Here with the best one thing it ever found,
As of my soul's best birthdays dawns the third.
There is a friend that as the wise man saith
Cleaves closer than a brother: nor to me
Hath time not shown, through days like waves at strife,
This truth more sure than all things else but death,
This pearl most perfect found in all the sea
That washes toward your feet these waifs of life.

THE PINES
April 1882

Index of Contents

Love, that is first and last of all things made,

The light that has the living world for shade,
The spirit that for temporal veil has on
The souls of all men woven in unison,
One fiery raiment with all lives inwrought
And lights of sunny and starry deed and thought,
And alway through new act and passion new
Shines the divine same body and beauty through,
The body spiritual of fire and light
That is to worldly noon as noon to night;
Love, that is flesh upon the spirit of man
And spirit within the flesh whence breath began;
Love, that keeps all the choir of lives in chime;
Love, that is blood within the veins of time;
That wrought the whole world without stroke of hand,
Shaping the breadth of sea, the length of land,
And with the pulse and motion of his breath
Through the great heart of the earth strikes life and death,
The sweet twain chords that make the sweet tune live
Through day and night of things alternative,
Through silence and through sound of stress and strife,
And ebb and flow of dying death and life:
Love, that sounds loud or light in all men's ears,
Whence all men's eyes take fire from sparks of tears,
That binds on all men's feet or chains or wings;
Love that is root and fruit of terrene things;
Love, that the whole world's waters shall not drown,
The whole world's fiery forces not burn down;
Love, that what time his own hands guard his head
The whole world's wrath and strength shall not strike dead;
Love, that if once his own hands make his grave
The whole world's pity and sorrow shall not save;
Love, that for very life shall not be sold,
Nor bought nor bound with iron nor with gold;
So strong that heaven, could love bid heaven farewell,
Would turn to fruitless and unflowering hell;
So sweet that hell, to hell could love be given,
Would turn to splendid and sonorous heaven;
Love that is fire within thee and light above,
And lives by grace of nothing but of love;
Through many and lovely thoughts and much desire
Led these twain to the life of tears and fire;
Through many and lovely days and much delight
Led these twain to the lifeless life of night.

Yea, but what then? albeit all this were thus,
And soul smote soul and left it ruinous,
And love led love as eyeless men lead men,
Through chance by chance to deathward—Ah, what then?

Hath love not likewise led them further yet,
out through the years where memories rise and set,
Some large as suns, some moon-like warm and pale
Some starry-sighted, some through clouds that sail
Seen as red flame through spectral float of fume,
Each with the blush of its own special bloom
On the fair face of its own coloured light,
Distinguishable in all the host of night,
Divisible from all the radiant rest
And separable in splendour? Hath the best
Light of love's all, of all that burn and move,
A better heaven than heaven is? Hath not love
Made for all these their sweet particular air
To shine in, their own beams and names to bear,
Their ways to wander and their wards to keep,
Till story and song and glory and all things sleep?
Hath he not plucked from death of lovers dead
Their musical soft memories, and kept red
The rose of their remembrance in men's eyes,
The sunsets of their stories in his skies,
The blush of their dead blood in lips that speak
Of their dead lives, and in the listener's cheek
That trembles with the kindling pity lit
In gracious hearts for some sweet fever-fit,
A fiery pity enkindled of pure thought
By tales that make their honey out of nought,
The faithless faith that lives without belief
Its light life through, the griefless ghost of grief?
Yea, as warm night refashions the sere blood
In storm-struck petal or in sun-struck bud,
With tender hours and tempering dew to cure
The hunger and thirst of day's distemperature
And ravin of the dry discolouring hours,
Hath he not bid relume their flameless flowers
With summer fire and heat of lamping song,
And bid the short-lived things, long dead, live long,
And thought remake their wan funereal fames,
And the sweet shining signs of women's names
That mark the months out and the weeks anew
He moves in changeless change of seasons through
To fill the days up of his dateless year
Flame from Queen Helen to Queen Guenevere?
For first of all the sphery signs whereby
Love severs light from darkness, and most high,
In the white front of January there glows
The rose-red sign of Helen like a rose:
And gold-eyed as the shore-flower shelterless
Whereon the sharp-breathed sea blows bitterness,

A storm-star that the seafarers of love
Strain their wind-wearied eyes for glimpses of,
Shoots keen through February's grey frost and damp
The lamplike star of Hero for a lamp;
The star that Marlowe sang into our skies
With mouth of gold, and morning in his eyes;
And in clear March across the rough blue sea
The signal sapphire of Alcyone
Makes bright the blown bross of the wind-foot year;
And shining like a sunbeam-smitten tear
Full ere it fall, the fair next sign in sight
Burns opal-wise with April-coloured light
When air is quick with song and rain and flame,
My birth-month star that in love's heaven hath name
Iseult, a light of blossom and beam and shower,
My singing sign that makes the song-tree flower;
Next like a pale and burning pearl beyond
The rose-white sphere of flower-named Rosamond
Signs the sweet head of Maytime; and for June
Flares like an angered and storm-reddening moon
Her signal sphere, whose Carthaginian pyre
Shadowed her traitor's flying sail with fire;
Next, glittering as the wine-bright jacinth-stone,
A star south-risen that first to music shone,
The keen girl-star of golden Juliet bears
Light northward to the month whose forehead wears
Her name for flower upon it, and his trees
Mix their deep English song with Veronese;
And like an awful sovereign chrysolite
Burning, the supreme fire that blinds the night,
The hot gold head of Venus kissed by Mars,
A sun-flower among small sphered flowers of stars,
The light of Cleopatra fills and burns
The hollow of heaven whence ardent August yearns;
And fixed and shining as the sister-shed
Sweet tears for Phaethon disorbed and dead,
The pale bright autumn's amber-coloured sphere,
That through September sees the saddening year
As love sees change through sorrow, hath to name
Francesca's; and the star that watches flame
The embers of the harvest overgone
Is Thisbe's, slain of love in Babylon,
Set in the golden girdle of sweet signs
A blood-bright ruby; last save one light shines
An eastern wonder of sphery chrysopras,
The star that made men mad, Angelica's;
And latest named and lordliest, with a sound
Of swords and harps in heaven that ring it round,

Last love-light and last love-song of the year's,
Gleams like a glorious emerald Guenevere's.
These are the signs wherethrough the year sees move,
Full of the sun, the sun-god which is love,
A fiery body blood-red from the heart
Outward, with fire-white wings made wide apart,
That close not and unclose not, but upright
Steered without wind by their own light and might
Sweep through the flameless fire of air that rings
From heaven to heaven with thunder of wheels and wings
And antiphones of motion-moulded rhyme
Through spaces out of space and timeless time.

So shine above dead chance and conquered change
The spherèd signs, and leave without their range
Doubt and desire, and hope with fear for wife,
Pale pains, and pleasures long worn out of life.
Yea, even the shadows of them spiritless,
Through the dim door of sleep that seem to press,
Forms without form, a piteous people and blind,
Men and no men, whose lamentable kind
The shadow of death and shadow of life compel
Through semblances of heaven and false-face hell,
Through dreams of light and dreams of darkness tost
On waves innavigable, are these so lost?
Shapes that wax pale and shift in swift strange wise,
Voice faces with unspeculative eyes,
Dim things that gaze and glare, dead mouths that move,
Featureless heads discrowned of hate and love,
Mockeries and masks of motion and mute breath,
Leavings of life, the superflux of death—
If these things and no more than these things be
Left when man ends or changes, who can see?
Or who can say with what more subtle sense
Their subtler natures taste in air less dense
A life less thick and palpable than ours,
Warmed with faint fires and sweetened with dead flowers
And measured by low music? how time fares
In that wan time-forgotten world of theirs,
Their pale poor world too deep for sun or star
To live in, where the eyes of Helen are,
And hers who made as God's own eyes to shine
The eyes that met them of the Florentine,
Wherein the godhead thence transfigured lit
All time for all men with the shadow of it?
Ah, and these too felt on them as God's grace
The pity and glory of this man's breathing face;
For these, too, these my lovers, these my twain,

Saw Dante, saw God visible by pain,
With lips that thundered and with feet that trod
Before men's eyes incognisable God;
Saw love and wrath and light and night and fire
Live with one life and one mouths respire,
And in one golden sound their whole soul heard
Sounding, one sweet immitigable word.

They have the night, who had like us the day;
We, whom day binds, shall have the night as they.
We, from the fetters of the light unbound,
Healed of our wound of living, shall sleep sound.
All gifts but one the jealous God may keep
From our soul's longing, one he cannot—sleep.
This, though he grudge all other grace to prayer,
This grace his closed hand cannot choose but spare.
This, though his hear be sealed to all that live,
Be it lightly given or lothly, God must give.
We, as the men whose name on earth is none,
We too shall surely pass out of the sun;
Out of the sound and eyeless light of things,
Wide as the stretch of life's time-wandering wings,
Wide as the naked world and shadowless,
And long-lived as the world's own weariness.
Us too, when all the fires of time are cold,
The heights shall hide us and the depths shall hold.
Us too, when all the tears of time are dry,
The night shall lighten from her tearless eye.
Blind is the day and eyeless all its light,
But the large unbewildered eye of night
Hath sense and speculation; and the sheer
Limitless length of lifeless life and clear,
The timeless space wherein the brief worlds move
Clothed with light life and fruitful with light love,
With hopes that threaten, and with fears that cease,
Past fear and hope, hath in it only peace.

Yet of these lives inlaid with hopes and fears,
Spun fine as fire and jewelled thick with tears,
These lives made out of loves that long since were,
Lives wrought as ours of earth and burning air,
Fugitive flame, and water of secret springs,
And clothed with joys and sorrows as with wings,
Some yet are good, if aught be good, to save
Some while from washing wreck and wrecking wave.
Was such not theirs, the twain I take, and give
Out of my life to make their dead life live
Some days of mine, and blow my living breath

Between dead lips forgotten even of death?
So many and many of old have given my twain
Love and live song and honey-hearted pain,
Whose root is sweetness and whose fruit is sweet,
So many and with such joy have tracked their feet,
What should I do to follow? yet I too,
I have the heart to follow, many or few
Be the feet gone before me; for the way,
Rose-red with remnant roses of the day
Westward, and eastward white with stars that break,
Between the green and foam is fair to take
For any sail the sea-wind steers for me
From morning into morning, sea to sea.

I

THE SAILING OF THE SWALLOW

About the middle music of the spring
Came from the castled shore of Ireland's king
A fair ship stoutly sailing, eastward bound
And south by Wales and all its wonders round
To the loud rocks and ringing reaches home
That take the wild wrath of the Cornish foam,
Past Lyonesse unswallowed of the tides
And high Carlion that now the steep sea hides
To the wind-hollowed heights and gusty bays
Of sheer Tintagel, fair with famous days.
Above the stem a gilded swallow shone,
Wrought with straight wings and eyes of glittering stone
As flying sunward oversea, to bear
Green summer with it through the singing air.
And on the deck between the rowers at dawn,
As the bright sail with brightening wind was drawn,
Sat with full face against the strengthening light
Iseult, more fair than foam or dawn was white.
Her gaze was glad past love's own singing of,
And her face lovely past desire of love.
Past thought and speech her maiden motions were,
And a more golden sunrise was her hair.
The very veil of her bright flesh was made
As of light woven and moonbeam-coloured shade
More fine than moonbeams; white her eyelids shone
As snow sun-stricken that endures the sun,
And through their curled and coloured clouds of deep
Luminous lashes thick as dreams in sleep

Shone as the sea's depth swallowing up the sky's
The springs of unimaginable eyes.
As the wave's subtler emerald is pierced through
With the utmost heaven's inextricable blue,
And both are woven and molten in one sleight
Of amorous colour and implicated light
Under the golden guard and gaze of noon,
So glowed their awless and amorous plenilune,
Azure and gold and ardent grey, made strange
With fiery difference and deep interchange
Inexplicable of glories multiform;
Now as the sullen sapphire swells toward storm
Foamless, their bitter beauty grew acold,
And now afire with ardour of fine gold.
Her flower-soft lips were meek and passionate,
For love upon them like a shadow sate
Patient, a foreseen vision of sweet things,
A dream with eyes fast shut and plumeless wings
That knew not what man's love or life should be,
Nor had it sight nor heart to hope or see
What thing should come, but childlike satisfied
Watched out its virgin vigil in soft pride
And unkissed expectation; and the glad
Clear cheeks and throat and tender temples had
Such maiden heat as if a rose's blood
Beat in the live heart of a lily-bud.
Between the small round breasts a white way led
Heavenward, and from slight foot to slender head
The whole fair body flower-like swayed and shone
Moving, and what her light hand leant upon
Grew blossom-scented: her warm arms began
To round and ripen for delight of man
That they should clasp and circle: her fresh hands,
Like regent lilies of reflowering lands
Whose vassal firstlings, crown and star and plume,
Bow down to the empire of that sovereign bloom,
Shone sceptreless, and from her face there went
A silent light as of a God content;
Save when, more swift and keen than love or shame,
Some flash of blood, light as the laugh of flame,
Broke it with sudden beam and shining speech,
As dream by dream shot through her eyes, and each
Outshone the last that lightened, and not one
Showed her such things as should be borne and done.
Though hard against her shone the sunlike face
That in all change and wreck of time and place
Should be the star of her sweet living soul.
Nor had love made it as his written scroll

For evil will and good to read in yet;
But smooth and mighty, without scar or fret,
Fresh and high-lifted was the helmless brow
As the oak-tree flower that tops the topmost bough,
Ere it drops off before the perfect leaf;
And nothing save his name he had of grief,
The name his mother, dying as he was born,
Made out of sorrow in very sorrow's scorn,
And set it on him smiling in her sight,
Tristram; who now, clothed with sweet youth and might,
As a glad witness wore that bitter name,
The second symbol of the world for fame.
Famous and full of fortune was his youth
Ere the beard's bloom had left his cheek unsmooth,
And in his face a lordship of strong joy
And height of heart no chance could curb or cloy
Lightened, and all that warmed them at his eyes
Loved them as larks that kindle as they rise
Toward light they turn to music love the blue strong skies.
So like the morning through the morning moved
Tristram, a light to look on and be loved.
Song spring between his lips and hands, and shone
Singing, and strengthened and sat down thereon
As a bird settles to the second flight,
Then from beneath his harping hands with might
Leapt, and made way and had its fill and died,
And all whose hearts were fed upon it sighed
Silent, and in them all the fire of tears
Burned as wine drunken not with lips but ears.
And gazing on his fervent hands that made
The might of music all their souls obeyed
With trembling strong subservience of delight
Full many a maid that had him once in sight
Thought in the secret rapture of her heart
In how dark onset had these hands borne part
How oft, and were so young and sweet of skill;
And those red lips whereon the song burned still,
What words and cries of battle had they flung
Athwart the swing and shriek of swords, so young;
And eyes as glad as summer, what strange youth
Fed them so full of happy heart and truth,
That had seen sway from side to sundering side
The steel flow of that terrible springtide
That the moon rules not, but the fire and light
Of men's hearts mixed in the mid mirth of fight.
Therefore the joy and love of him they had
Made thought more amorous in them and more glad
For his fame's sake remembered, and his youth

Gave his fame flowerlike fragrance and soft growth
As of a rose requickening, when he stood
Fair in their eye, a flower of faultless blood.
And that sad queen to whom his life was death,
A rose plucked forth of summer in mid breath,
A star fall'n out of season in mid throe
Of that life's joy that makes the star's life glow,
Made their love sadder toward him and more strong.
And in mid change of time and fight and song
Chance cast him westward on the low sweet strand
Where songs are sung of the old green Irish land,
And the sky loves it, and the sea loves best,
And as a bird is taken to man's breast
The sweet-souled land where sorrow sweetest sings
Is wrapt round with them as with hands and wings
And taken to the sea's heart as a flower.
There in the luck and light of his good hour
Came to the king's court like a noteless man
Tristram, and while some half a season ran
Abode before him harping in his hall,
And taught sweet craft of new things musical
To the dear maiden mouth and innocent hands
That for his sake are famous in all lands.
Yet was not love between them, for their fate
Lay wrapt in its appointed hour at wait,
And had no flower to show yet, and no string.
But once being vexed with some past wound the king
Bade give him comfort of sweet baths, and then
Should Iseult watch him as his handmaiden,
For his more honour in men's sight, and ease
The hurts he had with holy remedies
Made by her mother's magic in strange hours
Out of live roots and life-compelling flowers.
And finding by the wound's shape in his side
This was the knight by whom their strength had died
And all their might in one man overthrown
Had left their shame in sight of all men shown,
She would have slain him swordless with his sword;
Yet seemed he to her so great and fair a lord
She heaved up hand and smote not; then said he
Laughing—"What comfort shall this dead man be,
Damsel? what hurt is for my blood to heal?
But set your hand not near the toothèd steel
Lest the fang strike it."—"Yea, the fang," she said,
"Should it not sting the very serpent dead
That stung mine uncle? for his slayer art though,
And half my mother's heart is bloodless now
Through thee, that mad'st the veins of all her kin

Bleed in his wounds whose veins through thee ran thin."
Yet thought she how their hot chief's violent heart
Had flung the fierce word forth upon their part
Which bade to battle the best knight that stood
On Arthur's, and so dying of his wild mood
Had set upon his conqueror's flesh the seal
Of his mishallowed and anointed steel,
Whereof the venom and enchanted might
Made the sign burn here branded in her sight.
These things she stood recasting, and her soul
Subsiding till its wound of wrath were whole
Grew smooth again as thought still softening stole
Through all its tempered passion; nor might hate
Keep high the fire against him lit of late;
But softly from his smiling sight she passed.
And peace thereafter made between them fast
Made peace between two kingdoms, when he went
Home with hands reconciled and heart content,
To bring fair truce 'twixt Cornwall's wild bright strand
And the long wrangling wars of that loud land.
And when full peace was struck betwixt them twain
Forth must he fare by those green straits again,
And bring back Iseult for a plighted bride
And set to reign at Mark his uncle's side.
So now with feast made and all triumphs done
They sailed between the moonfall and the sun
Under the spent stars eastward; but the queen
Out of wise heart and subtle love had seen
Such things as might be, dark as in a glass,
And lest some doom of these should come to pass
Bethought her with her secret soul alone
To work some charm for marriage unison
And strike the heart of Iseult to her lord
With power compulsive more than stroke of sword.
Therefore with marvellous herbs and spells she wrought
To win the very wonder of her thought,
And brewed it with her secret hands and blest
And drew and gave out of her secret breast
To one her chosen and Iseult's handmaiden,
Brangwain, and bade her hide from sight of men
This marvel covered in a golden cup,
So covering in her heart the counsel up
As in the gold the wondrous win lay close;
And when the last shout with the last cup rose
About the bride and bridegroom bound to bed,
Then should this one world of her will be said
To her new-married maiden child, that she
Should drink with Mark this draught in unity,

And no lip touch it for her sake but theirs:
For with long love and consecrating prayers
The wine was hallowed for their mouths to pledge,
And if a drop fell from the beaker's edge
That drop should Iseult hold as dear as blood
Shed from her mother's heart to do her good.
And having drunk they twain should be one heart
Who were one flesh till fleshly death should part—
Death, who parts all. So Brangwain swore, and kept
The hid thing by her while she waked or slept.
And now they sat to see the sun again
Whose light of eye had looked on no such twain
Since Galahault in the rose-time of the year
Brought Launcelot first to sight of Guenevere.

And Tristram caught her changing eyes and said:
"As this day raises daylight from the dead
Might not this face the life of a dead man?"

And Iseult, gazing where the sea was wan
Out of the sun's way, said: "I pray you not
Praise me, but tell me there in Camelot,
Saving the queen, who hath most name of fair?
I would I were a man and dwelling there,
That I might win me better praise than yours,
Even such as you have; for your praise endures,
That with great deeds ye wring from mouths of men,
But ours—for shame, where is it? Tell me then,
Since woman may not wear a better here,
Who of this praise hath most save Guenevere?"

And Tristram, lightening with a laugh held in—
"Surely a little praise is this to win,
A poor praise and a little! but of these
Hapless, whom love serves only with bowed knees,
Of such poor women fairer face hath none
That lifts her eyes alive against the sun
Than Arthur's sister, whom the north seas call
Mistress of isles; so yet majestical
Above the crowns on younger heads she moves,
Outlightening with her eyes our late-born loves."

"Ah," said Iseult, "is she more tall than I?
Look, I am tall;" and struck the mast hard by,
With utmost reach of her bright hand;
"And look, fair lord, now, when I rise and stand,
How high with feet unlifted I can touch
Standing straight up; could this queen do thus much?

Nay, over tall she must be then, like me;
Less fair than lesser women. May this be,
That still she stands the second stateliest there,
So more than many so much younger fair,
She, born when yet the king your lord was not,
And has the third knight after Launcelot
And after you to serve her? nay, sir, then
God made her for a godlike sign to men."

"Ay," Tristram answered, "for a sign, a sign—
Would God it were not! for no planets shine
With half such fearful forecast of men's fate
As a fair face so more unfortunate."

Then with a smile that lit not on her brows
But moved upon her red mouth tremulous
Light as a sea-bird's motion oversea,
"Yea," quoth Iseult, "the happier hap for me,
With no such face to bring men no such fate.
Yet her might all we women born too late
Praise for good hap, who so enskied above
Not more in age excels us than man's love."

There came a glooming light on Tristram's face
Answering: "God keep you better in his grace
Than to sit down beside her in men's sight.
For if men be not blind whom God gives light
And lie not in whose lips he bids truth live,
Great grief shall she be given, and greater give.
For Merlin witnessed of her years ago
That she would work woe and should suffer woe
Beyond the race of women: and in truth
Her face, a spell that knows nor age nor youth,
Like youth being soft, and subtler-eyed than age,
With lips that mock the doom her eyes presage,
Hath on it such a light of cloud and fire,
With charm and change of keen or dim desire,
And over all a fearless look of fear
Hung like a veil across its changing cheer,
Make up of fierce foreknowledge and sharp scorn,
That it were better she had not been born.
For not love's self can help a face which hath
Such insubmissive anguish of wan wrath,
Blind prescience and self-contemptuous hate
Of her own soul and heavy-footed fate,
Writ broad upon its beauty: none the less
Its fire of bright and burning bitterness
Takes with as quick a flame the sense of men

As any sunbeam, nor is quenched again
With any drop of dewfall; yea, I think,
No herb of force or blood-compelling drink
Would heal a heart that ever it made hot.
Ay, and men too that greatly love her not,
Seeing the great love of her and Lamoracke,
Make no great marvel, nor look strangely back
When with his gaze about her she goes by
Pale as a breathless and star-quickening sky
Between the moonrise and sunset, and moves out
Clothed with the passion of his eyes about
As night with all her stars, yet night is black;
And she, clothed warm with love of Lamoracke,
Girt with his worship as with girdling gold,
Seems all at heart anhungered and acold,
Seems sad at heart and loveless of the light,
As night, star-clothed or naked, is but night."

And with her sweet yes sunken, and the mirth
Dead in their look as earth lies dead in earth
That reigned on earth and triumphed, Iseult said:
"Is it her shame of something done and dead
Or fear of something to be born and done
That so in her soul's eye puts out the sun?"

And Tristram answered: "Surely, as I think,
This gives her soul such bitterness to drink,
The sin born blind, the sightless sin unknown,
Wrought when the summer in her blood was blown
But scarce aflower, and spring first flushed her will
With bloom of dreams no fruitage should fulfil,
When out of vision and desire was wrought
The sudden sin that from the living thought
Leaps a live deed and dies not: then there came
On that blind sin swift eyesight light a flame
Touching the dark to death, and made her mad
With helpless knowledge that too late forbade
What was before the bidding: and she knew
How sore a life dead love should lead her through
To what sure end how fearful; and though yet
Nor with her blood nor tears her way be wet
And she look bravely with set face on fate,
Yet she knows well the serpent hour at wait
Somewhere to string and spare not; ay, and he,
Arthur"—
"The king," quoth Iseult suddenly,
"Doth the king too live so in sight of fear?
They say sin touches not a man so near

As shame a woman; yet he too should be
Part of the penance, being more deep than she
Set in the sin.
"Nay," Tristram said, "for thus
It fell by wicked hap and hazardous,
That wittingly he sinned no more than youth
May sin and be assoiled of God and truth,
Repenting; since in his first year of reign
As he stood splendid with his foemen slain
And light of new-blown battles, flushed and hot
With hope and life, came greeting from King Lot
Out of his wind-worn islands oversea,
And homage to my king and fealty
Of those north seas wherein the strange shapes swim,
As from his man; and Arthur greeted him
As his good lord and courteously, and bade
To his high feast; who coming with him had
This Queen Morgause of Orkney, his fair wife,
In the green middle Maytime of her life,
And scarce in April was our king's as then,
And goodliest was he of all flowering men,
And of what graft as yet himself know not;
But cold as rains in autumn was King Lot
And grey-grown out of season: so there sprang
Swift love between them, and all spring through sang
Light in their joyous hearing; for none knew
The bitter bond of blood between them two,
Twain fathers but one mother, till too late
The sacred mouth of Merlin set forth fate
And brake the secret seal on Arthur's birth,
And showed his ruin and his rule on earth
Inextricable, and light on lives to be.
For surely, though time slay us, yet shall we
Have such high name and lordship of good days
As shall sustain us living, and men's praise
Shall burn a beacon lit above us dead.
And of the king how shall not this be said
When any of us from any mouth has praise,
That such were men in only this king's days.
In Arthur's? yea, come shine or shade, no less
His name shall be one name with knightliness,
His fame one light with sunlight. Yet in sooth
His age shall bear the burdens of his youth
And bleed from his own bloodshed; for indeed
Blind to him blind his sister brought forth seed,
And of the child between them shall be born
Destruction: so shall God not suffer scorn,
Nor in men's souls and lives his law lie dead."

And as one moved and marvelling Iseult said:
"Great pity it is and strange it seems to me
God could not do them so much right as we,
Who slay not men for witless evil done;
And these the noblest under God's glad sun
For sin they knew not he that knew shall slay,
And smite blind men for stumbling in fair day.
What good is it to God that such should die?
Shall the sun's light grow sunnier in the sky
Because their light of spirit is clean put out?"

And sighing, she looked from wave to cloud about,
And even with that full-grown feet of day
Sprang upright on the quivering water-way,
And his face burned against her meeting face
Most like a lover's thrilled with great love's grace
Whose glance takes fire and gives; the quick sea shone
And shivered like spread wings of angels blown
By the sun's breath before him; and a low
Sweet gale shook all the foam-flowers of thin snow
As into rainfall of sea-roses shed
Leaf by wild leaf on that green garden-bed
Which tempests till and sea-winds turn and plough:
For rosy and fiery round the running prow
Fluttered the flakes and feathers of the spray,
And bloomed like blossoms cast by God away
To waste on the ardent water; swift the moon
Withered to westward as a face in swoon
Death-stricken by glad tidings: and the height
Throbbed and the centre quivered with delight
And the depth quailed with passion as of love,
Till like the heart of some new-mated dove
Air, light, and wave seemed full of burning rest,
With motion as of one God's beating breast.

And her heart sprang in Iseult, and she drew
With all her spirit and life the sunrise through
And through her lips the keen triumphant air
Sea-scented, sweeter than land-roses were,
And through her eyes the whole rejoicing east
Sun-satisfied, and all the heaven at feast
Spread for the morning; and the imperious mirth
Of wind and light that moved upon the earth,
Making the spring, and all the fruitful might
And strong regeneration of delight
That swells the seedling leaf and sapling man,
Since the first life in the first world began

To burn and burgeon through void limbs and veins,
And the first love with sharp sweet procreant pains
To pierce and bring forth roses; yea, she felt
Through her own soul the sovereign morning melt,
And all the sacred passion of the sun;
And as the young clouds flamed and were undone
About him coming, touched and burnt away
In rosy ruin and yellow spoil of day,
The sweet veil of her body and corporal sense
Felt the dawn also cleave it, and incense
With light from inward and with effluent heat
The kindling soul through fleshly hands and feet.
And as the august great blossom of the dawn
Burst, and the full sun scarce from sea withdrawn
Seemed on the fiery water a flower afloat,
So as a fire the mighty morning smote
Throughout her, and incensed with the influent hour
Her whole soul's one great mystical red flower
Burst, and the bud of her sweet spirit broke
Rose-fashion, and the strong spring at a stroke
Thrilled, and was cloven, and from the full sheath came
The whole rose of the woman red as flame:
And all her Mayday blood as from a swoon
Flushed, and May rose up in her and was June.
So for a space her hearth as heavenward burned:
Then with half summer in her eyes she turned,
And on her lips was April yet, and smiled,
As though the spirit and sense unreconciled
Shrank laughing back, and would not ere its hour
Let life put forth the irrevocable flower.

And the soft speech between them grew again
With questionings and records of what men
Rose mightiest, and what names for love or fight
Shone starriest overhead of queen or knight.
There Tristram spake of many a noble thing,
High feast and storm of tournay round the king,
Strange quest by perilous lands of marsh and brake
And circling woods branch-knotted like a snake
And places pale with sins that they had seen,
Where was no life of red fruit or of green
But all was as a dead face wan and dun;
And bowers of evil builders whence the sun
Turns silent, and the moon holds hardly light
Above them through the sick and star-crossed night;
And of their hands through whom such holds lay waste,
And all their strengths dishevelled and defaced
Fell ruinous, and were not from north to south:

And of the might of Merlin's ancient mouth,
The son of no man's loins, begot by doom
In speechless sleep out of a spotless womb;
For sleeping among graves where none had rest
And ominous houses of dead bones unblest
Among the grey grass rough as old rent hair
And wicked herbage whitening like despair
And blown upon with blasts of dolorous breath
From gaunt rare gaps and hollow doors of death,
A maid unspotted, senseless of the spell,
Felt not about her breathe some thing of hell
Whose child and hers was Merlin; and to him
Great light from God gave sight of all things dim
And wisdom of all wondrous things, to say
What root should bear what fruit of night or day,
And sovereign speech and counsel higher than man,
Wherefore his youth like age was wise and wan,
And his age sorrowful and fain to sleep;
Yet should sleep never, neither laugh nor weep,
Till in some depth of deep sweet land or sea
The heavenly hands of holier Nimue,
That was the nurse of Launcelot, and most sweet
Of all that move with magical soft feet
Among us, being of lovelier blood and breath,
Should shut him in with sleep as kind as death:
For she could pass between the quick and dead:
And of her love toward Pelleas, for whose head
Love-wounded and world-wearied she had won
A place beyond all pain in Avalon;
And of the fire that wasted afterward
The loveless eyes and bosom of Ettarde,
In whose false love his faultless heart had burned;
And now being rapt from her, her lost heart yearned
To seek him, and passed hungering out of life:
And after all the thunder-hours of strife
That roared between King Claudas and King Ban
How Nimue's mighty nursling waxed to man,
And how from his first field such grace he got
That all men's hearts bowed down to Launcelot,
And how the high prince Galahault held him dear
And led him even to love of Guenevere
And to that kiss which made break forth as fire
The laugh that was the flower of his desire,
The laugh that lightened at her lips for bliss
To win from Love so great a lover's kiss:
And of the toil of Balen all his days
To reap but thorns for fruit and tears for praise,
Whose hap was evil as his heart was good,

And all his works and ways by wold and wood
Led through much pain to one last labouring day
When blood for tears washed grief with life away:
And of the kin of Arthur, and their might;
The misborn head of Mordred, sad as night,
With cold waste cheeks and eyes as keen as pain,
And the close angry lips of Agravaine;
And gracious Gawain, scattering words as flowers,
The kindliest head of worldly paramours;
And the fair hand of Gareth, found in fight
Strong as a sea-beast's tushes and as white;
And of the king's self, glorious yet and glad
For all the toil and doubt of doom he had,
Clothed with men's loves and full of kingly days.

Then Iseult said: "Let each knight have his praise
And each good man good witness of his worth;
But when men laud the second name on earth,
Whom would they praise to have no worldly peer
Save him whose love makes glorious Guenevere?"

"Nay," Tristram said, "such man as he is none."
"What," said she, "there is none such under sun
Of all the large earth's living? yet I deemed
Men spake of one—but maybe men that dreamed,
Fools and tongue-stricken, witless, babbler's breed—
That for all high things was his peer indeed
Save this one highest, to be so loved and love."

And Tristram: "Little wit had these thereof;
For there is none such in the world as this."

"Ay, upon land," quoth Iseult, "none such is,
I doubt not, nor where fighting folk may be;
But were there none such between sky and sea,
The world's whole worth were poorer than I wist."

And Tristram took her flower-white hand and kissed,
Laughing; and through his fair face as in shame
The light blood lightened. "Hear they no such name?"
She said; and he, "If there be such a word,
I wot the queen's poor harper hath not heard."
Then, as the fuller-feathered hours grew long,
He help to speed their warm slow feet with song.

"Love, is it morning risen or night deceased
That makes the mirth of this triumphant east?
Is it bliss given or bitterness put by

That makes most glad men's hearts at love's high feast?
Grief smiles, joy weeps, that day should live and die.

"Is it with soul's thirst or with body's drouth
That summer yearns out sunward to the south,
With all the flowers that when thy birth drew nigh
Were molten in one rose to make thy mouth?
O love, what care though day should live and die?

"Is the sun glad of all love on earth,
The spirit and sense and work of things and worth?
Is the moon sad because the month must fly
And bring her death that can but bring back birth?
For all these things as day must live and die.

"Love, is it day that makes thee thy delight
Or thou that seest day made out of thy light?
Love, as the sun and sea are thou and I,
Sea without sun dark, sun without sea bright;
The sun is one though day should live and die.

"O which is elder, night or light, who knows?
And life or love, which first of these twain grows?
For life is born of love to wail and cry,
And love is born of life to heal his woes,
And light of night, that day should live and die.

"O sun of heaven above the worldly sea,
O very love, what light is this of thee!
My sea of soul is deep as thou art high,
But all thy light is shed through all of me,
As love's through love, while day shall live and die."

"Nay," said Iseult, "your song is hard to read."
"Ay?" said he: "or too light a song to heed,
Too slight to follow it may be? Who shall sing
Of love but as a churl before a king
If by love's worth men rate his worthiness?
Yet as the poor churl's worth to sing is less,
Surely the more shall be the great king's grace
To show for churlish love a kindlier face."
"No churl," she said, "but one in soothsayer's wise
Who tells but truths that help no more than lies.
I have heard men sing of love a simpler way
Than these wrought riddles made of night and day,
Like jewelled reins whereon the rhyme-bells hang."
And Tristram smiled and changed his song and sang.

"The breath between my lips of lips not mine,
Like spirit in sense that makes pure sense divine,
Is as life in them from the living sky
That entering fills my heart with blood of thine
And thee with me, while day shall live and die.

"Thy soul is shed into me with thy breath,
And in my heart each heartbeat of thee saith
How in thy life the lifesprings of me lie,
Even one life to be gathered of one death
In me and thee, though day may live and die.

"Ah, who knows now if in my veins it be
My blood that feels life sweet, or blood of thee,
And this thine eyesight kindled in mine eyes
That shows me in thy flesh the soul of me,
For thine made mine, while day may live and die?

"Ah, who knows yet if one be twain or one,
And sunlight separable again from sun,
And I from thee with all my lifesprings dry,
And thou from me with all thine heartbeats done,
Dead separate souls while day shall live and die?

"I see my soul within thine eyes, and hear
My spirit in all thy pulses thrill with fear,
And in my lips the passion of thee sigh,
And music of me made in mine own ear;
Am I not thou while day shall live and die?

"Art thou not I as I thy love am thou?
So let all things pass from us; we are now,
For all that was and will be, who knows why?
And all that is and is not, who knows how?
Who knows? God knows why day should live and die."

And Iseult mused and spake no word, but sought
Through all the hushed ways of her tongueless thought
What face or covered likeness of a face
In what veiled hour or dream-determined place
She seeing might take for love's face, and believe
This was the sprit to whom all spirits cleave.
For that sweet wonder of the twain made one
And each one twain, incorporate sun with sun,
Star with star molten, soul with soul imbued,
And all the soul's works, all their multitude,
Made one thought and one vision and one song,
Love—this thing, this, laid hand on her so strong

She could not choose but yearn till she should see.
So went she musing down her thoughts; but he,
Sweet-hearted as a bird that takes the sun
With clear strong eyes and feels the glad god run
Bright through his blood and wide rejoicing wings,
And opens all himself to heaven and sings,
Made her mind light and full of noble mirth
With words and songs the gladdest grown on earth,
Till she was blithe and high of heart as he.
So swam the Swallow through the springing sea

And while they sat at speech as at a feast,
Came a light wind fast hardening forth of the east
And blackening till its might had marred the skies;
And the sea thrilled as with heart-sundering sights
One after one drawn, with each breath it drew,
And the green hardened into iron blue,
And the soft light went out of all its face.
Then Tristram girt him for an oarsman's place
And took his oar and smote, and toiled with might
In the east wind's full face and the strong sea's spite
Labouring; and all the rowers rowed hard, but he
More mightily than any wearier three.
And Iseult watched him rowing with sinless eyes
That loved him but in holy girlish wise
For noble joy in his fair manliness
And trust and tender wonder; none the less
She thought if God had given her grace to be
Man, and make war on danger of earth and sea,
Even such a man she would be; for his stroke
Was mightiest as the mightier water broke,
And in sheer measure like strong music drave
Clean through the wet weight of the wallowing wave;
And as a tune before a great king played
For triumph was the tune their strong strokes made,
And sped the ship through which smooth strife of oars
Over the mid sea's grey foam-paven floors,
For all the loud breach of the waves at will.
So for an hour they fought the storm out still,
And the shorn foam spun from the blades, and high
The keel sprang from the wave-ridge, and the sky
Glared at them for a breath's space through the rain;
Then the bows with a sharp shock plunged again
Down, and the sea clashed on them, and so rose
The bright stem like one panting from swift blows,
And as a swimmer's joyous beaten head
Rears itself laughing, so in that sharp stead
The light ship lifted her long quivering bows

As might the man his buffeted strong brows
Out of the wave-breach; for with one stroke yet
Went all men's oars together, strongly set
As to loud music, and with hearts uplift
They smote their strong way through the drench and drift:
Till the keen hour had chafed itself to death
And the east wind fell fitfully, breath by breath,
Tired; and across the thin and slackening rain
Sprang the face southward of the sun again.
Then all they rested and were eased at heart;
And Iseult rose up where she sat apart,
And with her sweet soul deepening her deep eyes
Cast the furs from her and subtle embroideries
That wrapped her from the storming rain and spray,
And shining like all April in one day,
Hair, face, and throat dashed with the straying showers,
She stood the first of all the whole world's flowers,
And laughed on Tristram with her eyes, and said,
"I too have heart then, I was not afraid."
And answering some light courteous word of grace
He saw her clear face lighten on his face
Unwittingly, with unenamoured eyes
For the last time. A live man in such wise
Looks in the deadly face of his fixed hour
And laughs with lips wherein he hath no power
To keep the life yet some five minutes' space.
So Tristram looked on Iseult face to face
and knew not, and she knew not. The last time —
The last that should be told in any rhyme
Heard anywhere on mouths of singing men
That ever should sing praise of them again;
The last hour of their hurtless hearts at rest,
The last that peace should touch them, breast to breast,
The last that sorrow far from them should sit,
This last was with them, and they knew not it.

For Tristram being athirst with toil now spake,
Saying, "Iseult, for all dear love's labour's sake
Give me to drink, and give me for a pledge
The touch of four lips on the beaker's edge."
And Iseult sought and would not wake Brangwain
Who slept as one half dead with fear and pain,
Being tender-natured; so with hushed light feet
Went Iseult round her, with soft looks and sweet
Pitying her pain; so sweet a spirited thing
She was, and daughter of a kindly king.
And spying what strange bright secret charge was kept
Fast in the maid's white bosom while she slept,

She sought and drew the gold cup forth and smiled
Marvelling, with such light wonder as a child
That hears of glad sad life in magic lands;
And bare it back to Tristram with pure hands
Holding the love-draught that should be for flame
To burn out of them fear and faith and shame,
And lighten all their life up in men's sight,
And make them sad for ever. Then the knight
Bowed toward her and craved whence had she this strange thing
That might be spoil of some dim Asian king,
But starlight stolen from some waste place of sands,
And a maid bore it here in harmless hands.
And Iseult, laughing — "Other lords that be
Feast, and their men feast after them; but we,
Our men must keep the best wine back to feast
Till they be full and we of all men least
Feed after them and fain to fare so well:
So with mine handmaid and your squire it fell
That hid this bright thing from us in a wile:"
And with light lips yet full of their swift smile,
And hands that wist not though they dug a grave,
Undid the hasps of gold, and drank, and gave,
And he drank after, a deep glad kingly draught:
And all their life changed in them, for they quaffed
Death; if it be death so to drink, and fare
As men who change and are what these twain were.
And shuddering with eyes full of fear and fire
And heart-stung with a serpentine desire
He turned and saw the terror in her eyes
That yearned upon him shining in such wise
As a star midway in the midnight fixed.

Their Galahault was the cup, and she that mixed;
Nor other hand there needed, nor sweet speech
To lure their lips together; each on each
Hung with strange eyes and hovered as a bird
Wounded, and each mouth trembled for a word;
Their heads neared, and their hands were drawn in one,
And they saw dark, though still the unsunken sun
Far through fine rain shot fire into the south;
And their four lips became one burning mouth.

II

THE QUEEN'S PLEASANCE

Out of the night arose the second day,
And saw the ship's bows break the shoreward spray
As the sun's boat of gold and fire began
To sail the sea of heaven unsailed of man,
And the soft waves of sacred air to break
Round the prow launched into the morning's lake,
They saw the sign of their sea-travel done.

Ah, was not something seen of yester-sun,
When the sweet light that lightened all the skies
Saw nothing fairer than one maiden's eyes,
That whatsoever in all time's years may be
To-day's sun nor to-morrow's sun shall see?
Not while she lives, not when she comes to die,
Shall she look sunward with that sinless eye.

Yet fairer now than song may show them stand
Tristram and Iseult, hand in amorous hand,
Soul-satisfied, their eyes made great and bright
With all the love of all the livelong night;
With all its hours yet singing in their ears
No mortal music made of thoughts and tears,
But such a song, past conscience of man's thought.
As hearing he grows god and knows it not.
Nought else they saw nor heard but what the night
Had left for seal upon their sense and sight,
Sound of past pulses beating, fire of amorous light
Enough, and overmuch, and never yet
Enough, though love still hungering feed and fret,
To fill the cup of night which dawn must overset.
For still their eyes were dimmer than with tears
And dizzier from diviner sounds their ears
Than though from choral thunders of the quiring spheres.
They heard not how the landward waters rang,
Nor saw where high into the morning sprang,
Riven from the shore and bastioned with the sea,
Toward summits where the north wind's nest might be,
A wave-walled palace with its eastern gate
Full of the sunrise now and wide at wait,
And on the mighty-moulded stairs that clomb
Sheer from the fierce lip of the lapping foam
The knights of Mark that stood before the wall.
So with loud joy and storm of festival
They brought the bride in up the towery way
That rose against the rising front of day,
Stair based on stair, between the rocks unhewn,
To those strange halls wherethrough the tidal tune
Rang loud or lower from soft or strengthening sea,

Tower shouldering tower, to windward and to lee,
With change of floors and stories, flight on flight,
That clomb and curled up to the crowning height
Whence men might see wide east and west in one
And on one sea waned moon and mounting sun.
And severed from the sea-rock's base, where stand
Some worn walls yet they saw the broken strand,
The beachless cliff that in the sheer sea dips,
The sleepless shore inexorable to ships,
And the straight causeway's bare gaunt spine between
The sea-spanned walls and naked mainland's green.

On the mid stairs, between the light and dark,
Before the main tower's portal stood King Mark,
Crowned: and his face was as the face of one
Long time athirst and hungering for the sun
In barren thrall of bitter bonds, who now
Thinks here to feel its blessing on his brow.
A swart lean man, but kinglike, still of guise,
With black streaked beard and cold unquiet eyes,
Close-mouthed, gaunt-cheeked, wan as a morning moon,
Though hardly time on his worn hair had strewn
The thin first ashes from a sparing hand:
Yet little fire there burnt upon the brand,
And way-worn seemed he with life's wayfaring.
So between shade and sunlight stood the king,
And his face changed nor yearned not toward his bride;
But fixed between mild hope and patient pride
Abode what gift of rare or lesser worth
This day might bring to all his days on earth.
But at the glory of her when she came
His heart endured not: very fear and shame
Smote him, to take her by the hand and kiss,
Till both were molten in the burning bliss.
And with a thin flame flushing his cold face
He led her silent to the bridal place.
There were they wed and hallowed of the priest,
And all the loud time of the marriage feast
One thought within three hearts was as a fire,
Where craft and faith took counsel with desire.
For when the feast had made a glorious end
They gave the new queen for her maids to tend
At dawn of bride-night, and thereafter bring
With marriage music to the bridegroom king.
Then by device of craft between them laid
To him went Brangwain delicately, and prayed
That this thing even for love's sake might not be,
But without sound or light or eye to see

She might come in to bride-bed: and he laughed,
As one that wist not well of wise love's craft,
And bade all bridal things be as she would.
Yet of his gentleness he gat not good;
For clothed and covered with the nuptial dark
Soft like a bride came Brangwain to King Mark,
And to the queen came Tristram; and the night
Fled, and ere danger of detective light
From the king sleeping Brangwain slid away,
And where had lain her handmaid Iseult lay.
And the king waking saw beside his head
That face yet passion-coloured, amorous red
From lips not his, and all that strange hair shed
Across the tissued pillows, fold on fold,
Innumerable, incomparable, all gold,
To fire men's eyes with wonder, and with love
Men's hearts; so shone its flowering crown above
The brows enwound with that imperial wreath,
And framed with fragrant radiance round the face beneath.

And the king marvelled, seeing with sudden start
Her very glory, and said out of his heart;
"What have I done of good for God to bless
That all this he should give me, tress on tress,
All this great wealth and wondrous? Was it this
That in mine arms I had all night to kiss,
And mix with me this beauty? this that seems
More fair than heaven doth in some tired saint's dreams,
Being part of that same heaven? yea, more, for he,
Though loved of God so, yet but seems to see,
But to me sinful such great grace is given
That in mine hands I hold this part of heaven,
Not to mine eyes lent merely. Doth God make
Such things so godlike for man's mortal sake?
Have I not sinned, that in this fleshly life
Have made of her a mere man's very wife?"

So the king mused and murmured; and she heard
The faint sound trembling of each breathless word,
And laughed into the covering of her hair.

And many a day for many a month as fair
Slid over them like music; and as bright
Burned with love's offerings many a secret night.
And many a dawn and many a fiery noon
Blew prelude, when the horn's heart-kindling tune
Lit the live woods with sovereign sound of mirth
Before the mightiest huntsman hailed on earth

Lord of its lordliest pleasure, where he rode
Hard by her rein whose peerless presence glowed
Not as that white queen's of the virgin hunt
Once, whose crown-crescent braves the night-wind's brunt,
But with the sun for frontlet of a queenlier front.
For where the flashing of her face was turned
As lightning was the fiery light that burned
From eyes and brows enkindled more with speed
And rapture of the rushing of her steed
That once with only beauty; and her mouth
Was as a rose athirst that pants for drouth
Even while it laughs for pleasure of desire,
And all her heart was as a leaping fire.
Yet once more joy they took of woodland ways
Than came of all those flushed and fiery days
When the loud air was mad with life and sound,
Through many a dense green mile, of horn and hound
Before the king's hunt going along the wind,
And ere the timely leaves were changed or thinned,
Even in mid maze of summer. For the knight
Forth was once ridden toward some frontier fight
Against the lewd folk of the Christless lands
That warred with wild and intermittent hands
Against the king's north border; and there came
A knight unchristened yet of unknown name,
Swart Palamede, upon a secret quest,
To high Tintagel, and abode as guest
In likeness of a minstrel with the king.
Nor was there man could sound so sweet a string,
Save Tristram only, of all held best on earth.
And one loud eve, being full of wine and mirth,
Ere sunset left the walls and waters dark,
To that strange minstrel strongly swore King Mark,
By all that makes a knight's faith firm and strong,
That he for guerdon of his harp and song
Might crave and have his liking. Straight there came
Up the swart cheek a flash of swarthier flame
And the deep eyes fulfilled of glittering night
Laughed out in lightnings of triumphant light
As the grim harper spake: "O king, I crave
No gift of man that king may give to slave,
But this thy crowned queen only, this thy wife,
Whom yet unseen I loved, and set my life
On this poor chance to compass, even as here,
Being fairer famed than all save Guenevere."
Then as the noise of seaward storm that mocks
With roaring laughter from reverberate rocks
The cry from ships near shipwreck, harsh and high

Rose all the wrath and wonder in one cry
Through all the long roof's hollow depth and length
That hearts of strong men kindled in their strength
May speak in laughter lion-like, and cease,
Being wearied: only two men held their peace
And each glared hard on other: but King Mark
Spake first of these: "Man, though thy craft be dark
And thy mind evil that begat this thing,
Yet stands the word once plighted of a king
Fast: and albeit less evil it were for me
To give my life up than my wife, or be
A landless man crowned only with a curse,
Yet this in God's and all men's sight were worse,
To live soul-shamed a man of broken troth,
Abhorred of men as I abhor mine oath
Which yet I may forswear not." And he bowed
His head, and wept: and all men wept aloud,
Save one, that heard him weeping: but the queen
Wept not: and statelier yet than eyes had seen
That ever looked upon her queenly state
She rose, and in her eyes her heart was great
And full of wrath seen manifest and scorn
More strong than anguish to go thence forlorn
Of all men's comfort and her natural right.
And they went forth into the dawn of night.
Long by wild ways and clouded light they rode,
Silent; and fear less keen at heart abode
With Iseult than with Palamede: for awe
Constrained him, and the might of love's high law,
That can make lewd men loyal; and his heart
Yearned on her, if perchance with amorous art
And soothfast skill of very love he might
For courtesy find favour in her sight
And comfort of her mercies: for he wist
More grace might come of that sweet mouth unkissed
Than joy for violence done it, that should make
His name abhorred for shame's disloyal sake.
And in the stormy starlight clouds were thinned
And thickened by short gusts of changing wind
That panted like a sick man's fitful breath:
And like a moan of lions hurt to death
Came the sea's hollow noise along the night.
But ere its gloom from aught but foam had light
They halted, being aweary: and the knight
As reverently forbore her where she lay
As one that watched his sister's sleep till day.
Nor durst he kiss or touch her hand or hair
For love and shamefast pity, seeing how fair

She slept, and fenceless from the fitful air.
And shame at heart stung nigh to death desire,
But grief at heart burned in him like a fire
For hers and his own sorrowing sake, that had
Such grace for guerdon as makes glad men sad,
To have their will and want it. And the day
Sprang: and afar along the wild waste way
They heard the pulse and press of hurrying horse hoofs play:
And like the rushing of a ravenous flame
Whose wings make tempest of the darkness, came
Upon them headlong as in thunder borne
Forth of the darkness of the labouring morn
Tristram: and up forthright upon his steed
Leapt, as one blithe of battle, Palamede,
And mightily with shock of horse and man
They lashed together: and fair that fight began
As fair came up that sunrise: to and fro,
With knees night staggered and stout heads bent low
From each quick shock of spears on either side,
Reeled the strong steeds heavily, haggard-eyed
And heartened high with passion of their pride
As sheer the stout spears shocked again, and flew
Sharp-splintering: then, his sword as each knight drew,
They flashed and foined full royally, so long
That but to see so fair a strife and strong
A man might well have given out of his life
One year's void space forlorn of love or strife.
As when a bright north-easter, great of heart,
Scattering the strengths of squadrons, hurls apart
Ship from ship labouring violently, in such toil
As earns but ruin — with even so strong recoil
Back where the steeds hurled from the spear-shock, fain
And foiled of triumph: then with tightened rein
And stroke of spur, inveterate, either knight
Bore in again upon his foe with might,
Heart-hungry for the hot-mouthed feast of fight
And all athirst of mastery: but full soon
The jarring notes of that tempestuous tune
Fell, and its mighty music made of hands
Contending, clamorous through the loud waste lands,
Broke at once off; and shattered from his steed
Fell, as a mainmast ruining, Palamede,
Stunned: and those lovers left him where he lay,
And lightly through green lawns they rode away.

There was a bower beyond man's eye more fair
Than ever summer dews and sunniest air
Fed full with rest and radiance till the boughs

Had wrought a roof as for a holier house
Than aught save love might breathe in; fairer far
Than keeps the sweet light back of moon and star
From high king's chambers: there might love and sleep
Divide for joy the darkling hours, and keep
With amorous alternation of sweet strife
The soft and secret ways of death and life
Made smooth for pleasure's feet to rest and run
Even from the moondawn to the kindling sun,
Made bright for passion's feet to run and rest
Between the midnight's and the morning's breast,
Where hardly though her happy head lie down
It may forget the hour that wove its crown;
Where hardly though her joyous limbs be laid
They may forget the mirth that midnight made.
And thither, ere sweet night had slain sweet day,
Iseult and Tristram took their wandering way,
And rested, and refreshed their hearts with cheer
In hunters' fashion of the woods; and here
More sweet it seemed, while this might be, to dwell
And take of all world's weariness farewell
Than reign of all world's lordship queen and king.
Nor here would time for three moon's changes bring
Sorrow nor thought of sorrow; but sweet earth
Fostered them like her babes of eldest birth,
Reared warm in pathless woods and cherished well.
And the sun sprang above the sea and fell,
And the stars rose and sank upon the sea;
And outlaw-like, in forest wise and free,
The rising and the setting of their lights
Found those twain dwelling all those days and nights.
And under change of sun and star and moon
Flourished and fell the chaplets woven of June,
And fair through fervours of the deepening sky
Panted and passed the hours that lit July,
And each day blessed them out of heaven above,
And each night crowned them with the crown of love.
Nor till the might of August overhead
Weighed on the world was yet one roseleaf shed
Of all their joy's warm coronal, nor aught
Touched them in passing ever with a thought
That ever this might end on any day
Or any night not love them where they lay;
But like a babbling tale of barren breath
Seemed all report and rumour held of death,
And a false bruit the legend tear impearled
That such a thing as change was in the world.
And each bright song upon his lips that came,

Mocking the powers of change and death by name,
Blasphemed their bitter godhead, and defied
Time, though clothed round with ruin as kings with pride,
To blot the glad life out of love: and she
Drank lightly deep of his philosophy
In that warm wine of amorous words which is
Sweet with all truths of all philosophies.
For well he wist all subtle ways of song,
And in his soul the secret eye was strong
That burns in meditation, till bright words
Break flamelike forth as notes from fledgeling birds
That feel the soul speak through them of the spring
So fared they night and day as queen and king
Crowned of a kingdom wide as day and night.
Nor ever cloudlet swept or swam in sight
Across the darkling depths of their delight
Whose stars no skill might number, nor man's art
Sound the deep stories of its heavenly heart.
Till, even for wonder that such life should live,
Desires and dreams of what death's self might give
Would touch with tears and laughter and wild speech
The lips and eyes of passion, fain to reach,
Beyond all bourne of time or trembling sense,
The verge of love's last possible eminence.
Out of the heaven that storm nor shadow mars,
Deep from the starry depth beyond the stars,
A yearning ardour without scope or name
Fell on them, and the bright night's breath of flame
Shot fire into their kisses; and like fire
The lit dews lightened on the leaves, as higher
Night's heart beat on toward midnight. Far and fain
Somewhiles the soft rush of rejoicing rain
Solaced the darkness, and from steep to steep
Of heaven they saw the sweet sheet lightning leap
And laugh its heart out in a thousand smiles,
When the clear sea for miles on glimmering miles
Burned as though dawn were strewn abroad astray,
Or, showering out of heaven, all heaven's array
Had paven instead the waters: fain and far
Somewhiles the burning love of star for star
Spake words that love might well-nigh seem to hear
In such deep hours as turn delight to fear
Sweet as delight's self ever. So they lay
Tranced once, nor watched along the fiery bay
The shine of summer darkness palpitate and play.
She had nor sight nor voice; her swooning eyes
Knew not if night or light were in the skies;
Across her beauty sheer the moondawn shed

Its light as on a thing as white and dead;
Only with stress of soft fierce hands she prest
Between the throbbing blossoms of her breast
His ardent face, and through his hair her breath
Went quivering as when life is hard on death;
And with strong trembling fingers she strained fast
His head into her bosom; till at last
Satiate with sweetness of that burning bed,
His eyes afire with tears, he raised his head
And laughed into her lips; and all his heart
Filled hers; then face from face fell, and apart
Each hung on each with panting lips, and felt
Sense into sense and spirit in spirit melt.

"Hast thou no sword? I would not live till day,
O love, this night and we must pass away,
It must die soon, and let not us die late."

"Take then my sword and slay me; nay, but wait
Till day be risen; what, wouldst thou think to die
Before the light take hold upon the sky?"

"Yea, love; for how shall we have twice, being twain,
This very night of love's most rapturous reign?
Live thou and have thy day, and year by year
Be great, but what shall I be? Slay me here;
Let me die not when love lies dead, but now
Strike through my heart: nay, sweet, what heart hast thou?
Is it so much I ask thee, and spend my breath
In asking? nay, thou knowest it is but death.
Hadst thou true heart to love me, thou wouldst give
This: but for hate's sake thou swilt let me live."

Here he caught up her lips with his, and made
The wild prayer silent in her heart that prayed,
And strained her to him till all her faint breath sank
And her bright light limbs palpitated and shrank
And rose and fluctuated as flowers in rain
That bends them and they tremble and rise again
And heave and straighten and quiver all through with bliss
And turn afresh their mouths up for a kiss,
Amorous, athirst of that sweet influent love;
So, hungering towards his hovering lips above,
Her red-rose mouth yearned silent, and her eyes
Closed, and flashed after, as through June's darkest skies
The divine heartbeats of the deep live light
Make open and shut the gates of the outer night.

Long lay they still, subdued with love, nor knew
If could or light changed colour as it grew,
If star or moon beheld them; if above
The heaven of night waxed fiery with their love,
Or earth beneath were moved at heart and root
To burn as they, to burn and bright forth fruit
Unseasonable for love's sake; if tall trees
Bowed, and close flowers yearned open, and the breeze
Failed and fell silent as a flame that fails:
And all that hour unheard the nightingales
Clamoured, and all the woodland soul was stirred,
And depth and height were one great song unheard,
As though the world caught music and took fire
From the instant heart alone of their desire.

So sped their night of nights between them: so,
For all fears past and shadows, shine and snow,
That one pure hour all-golden where they lay
Made their life perfect and their darkness day.
And warmer waved its harvest yet to reap,
Till in the lovely fight of love and sleep
At length had sleep the mastery; and the dark
Was lit with soft live gleams they might not mark,
Fleet butterflies, each like a dead flower's ghost,
White, blue, and sere leaf-coloured; but the most
White as the sparkle of snow-flowers in the sun
Ere with his breath they lie at noon undone.
Whose kiss devours their tender beauty, and leaves
But raindrops on the grass and sere thin leaves
That were engraven with traceries of the snow
Flowerwise ere any flower of earth's would blow;
So swift they sprang and sank, so sweet and light
They swam the deep dim breathless air of night.
Now on her rose-white amorous breast half bare,
Now on her slumberous love-dishevelled hair,
The white wings lit and vanished, and afresh
Lit soft as snow lights on her snow-soft flesh,
On hand or throat or shoulder; and she stirred
Sleeping, and spake some tremulous bright word,
And laughed upon some dream too sweet for truth,
Yet not so sweet as very love and youth
That there had charmed her eyes to sleep at last.
Nor woke they till the perfect night was past,
And the soft sea thrilled with blind hope of light.
But ere the dusk had well the sun in sight
He turned and kissed her eyes awake and said,
Seeing earth and water neither quick nor dead
And twilight hungering toward the day to be,

"As the dawn loves the sunlight I love thee."
And even as rays with cloudlets in the skies
Confused in brief love's bright contentious wise,
Sleep strove with sense rekindling in her eyes;
And as the flush of birth scarce overcame
The pale pure pearl of unborn light with flame
Soft as may touch the rose's heart with shame
To break not all reluctant out of bud,
Stole up her sleeping cheek her waking blood;
And with the lovely laugh of love that takes
The whole soul prisoner ere the whole sense wakes,
Her lips for love's sake bade love's will be done.
And all the sea lay subject to the sun.

III

TRISTRAM IN BRITTANY

"'As the dawn loves the sunlight I love thee;'
As men that shall be swallowed of the sea
Love the sea's lovely beauty, as the night
That wanes before it loves the young sweet light,
And dies of loving; as the worn-out noon
Loves twilight, and as twilight loves the moon
That on its grave a silver seal shall set —
We have loved and slain each other, and love yet.
Slain; for we live not surely, being in twain:
In her I lived, and in me she is slain,
Who loved me that I brought her to her doom,
Who loved her that her love might be my tomb.
As all the streams of earth and all fresh springs
And sweetest waters, every brook that sings,
Each fountain where the young year dips its wings
First, and the first-fledged branches of it wave,
Even with one heart's love seek one bitter grave.
From hills that first see bared the morning's breast
And heights the sun last yearns to from the west,
All tend but toward the sea, all born most high
Strive downward, passing all things joyous by,
Seek to it and cast their lives in it and die
So strive all lives for death which all lives win;
So sought her soul to my soul, and therein
Was poured and perished: O my love, and mine
Sought to thee and died of thee and died as thine.
As the dawn loves the sunlight that must cease
Ere dawn again may rise and pass in peace;
Must die that she being dead may live again,

To be by his new rising nearly slain.
So rolls the great wheel of the great world round,
And no change in it and no fault is found,
And no true life of perdurable breath,
And surely no irrevocable death.
Day after day night comes that day may break,
And day comes back for night's reiterate sake.
Each into each dies, each of each is born:
Day past is night, shall night past not be morn?
Out of this moonless and faint-hearted night
That love yet lives in, shall there not be light?
Light strong as love, that love may live in yet?
Alas, but how shall foolish hope forget
How all these loving things that kill and die
Meet not but for a breath's space and pass by?
Night is kissed once of dawn and dies, and day
But touches twilight and is rapt away.
So may my love and her love meet once more,
And meeting be divided as of yore.
Yea, surely as the day-star loves the sun
And when he hath risen is utterly undone,
So is my love of her and hers of me—
And its most sweetness bitter as the sea.
Would God yet dawn might see the sun and die!"

Three years had looked on earth and passed it by
Since Tristram looked on Iseult, when he stood
So communing with dreams of evil and good,
And let all sad thoughts through his spirit sweep
As leaves through air or tears through eyes that weep
Or snowflakes through dark weather: and his soul,
That had seen all those sightless seasons roll
One after one, wave over weary wave,
Was in him as a corpse is in its grave.
Yet, for his heart was mighty, and his might
Through all the world as a great sound and light,
The mood was rare upon him; save that here
In the low sundawn of the lightening year
With all last year's toil and its triumph done
He could not choose but yearn for that set sun
Which at this season was the firstborn kiss
That made his lady's mouth one fire with his.
Yet his great heart being greater than his grief
Kept all the summer of his strength in leaf
And all the rose of his sweet spirit in flower;
Still his soul fed upon the sovereign hour
That had been or that should be; and once more
He looked through drifted sea and drifting shore

That crumbled in the wave-breach, and again
Spake sad and deep within himself: "What pain
Should make a man's soul wholly break and die,
Sapped as weak sand by water? How shall I
Be less than all less things are that endure
And strive and yield when time is? Nay, full sure
All these and we are parts of one same end;
And if through fire or water we twain tend
To that sure life where both must be made one,
If one we be, what matter? Thou, O sun,
The face of God, if God thou be not—nay,
What but God should I think thee, what should say,
Seeing thee rerisen, but very God?—should I,
I fool, rebuke thee sovereign in thy sky,
The clouds dead round thee and the air alive,
The winds that lighten and the waves that strive
Toward this shore as to that beneath thy breath,
Because in me my thoughts bear all towards death?
O sun, that when we are dead wilt rise as bright,
Air deepening up toward heaven, and nameless light,
And heaven immeasurable, and faint clouds blown
Between us and the lowest aerial zone
And each least skirt of their imperial state —
Forgive us that we held ourselves so great!
What should I do to curse you? I indeed
Am a thing meaner than this least wild weed
That my foot bruises and I know not — yet
Would not be mean enough for worms to fret
Before their time and mine was.
"Ah, and ye
Light washing weeds, blind waifs of dull blind sea,
Do ye so thirst and hunger and aspire,
Are ye so moved with such long strong desire
In the ebb and flow of your sad life, and strive
Still toward some end ye shall not see alive —
But at high noon ye know it by light and heat
Some half-hour, till ye feel the fresh tide beat
Up round you, and at night's most bitter noon
The ripples leave you naked to the moon?
And this dim dusty heather that I tread,
These half-born blossoms, born at once and dead,
Sere brown as funeral cloths, and purple as pall,
What if some life and grief be in them all?

"Ay, what of these? but, O strong sun! O sea!
I bid not you, divine things! comfort me,
I stand no up to match you in your sight—
Who hath said ye have mercy toward us, ye who have might?

And though ye had mercy, I think I would not pray
That ye should change your counsel or your way
To make our life less bitter: if such power
Be given the stars on one deciduous hour,
And such might be in planets to destroy
Grief and rebuild, and break and build up joy,
What man would stretch forth hand on them to make
Fate mutable, God foolish, for his sake?
For if in life or death be aught of trust,
And if some unseen just God or unjust
Put soul into the body of natural things
And in time's pauseless feet and worldwide wings
Some spirit of impulse and some sense of will
That steers them through the seas of good and ill
To some incognizable and actual end,
Be it just or unjust, foe to man or friend,
How should we make the stable spirit to swerve,
How teach the strong soul of the world to serve,
The imperious will in time and sense in space
That gives man life turn back to give man place —
The conscious law lose conscience of its way,
The rule and reason fail from night and day,
The stream flow back toward whence the springs began,
That less of thirst might sear the lips of man?
Let that which is be, and sure strength stand sure,
And evil or good and death or life endure,
Not alterable and rootless, but indeed
A very stem born of a very seed
That brings forth fruit in season: how should this
Die that was sown, and that not be which is,
And the old fruit change that came of the ancient root,
And he that planted bid it not bear fruit,
And he that watered smite his vine with drouth
Because its grapes are bitter in our mouth,
And he that kindled quench the sun with night
Because its beams are fire against our sight,
And he that tuned untune the sounding spheres
Because their song is thunder in our ears?
How should the skies change and the stars, and time
Break the large concord of the years that chime,
Answering, as wave to wave beneath the moon
That draws them shoreward, mar the whole tide's tune
For the instant foam's sake on one turning wave —
For man's sake that is grass upon a grave?
How should the law that knows not soon or late,
For whom no time nor space is — how should fate,
That is not good nor evil, wise nor mad,
Nor just nor unjust, neither glad nor sad —

How should the one thing that hath being, the one
That moves not as the stars move or the sun
Or any shadow or shape that lives or dies
In likeness of dead earth or living skies,
But its own darkness and its proper light
Clothe it with other names than day or night,
And its own soul of strength and spirit of breath
Feed it with other powers than life or death —
How should it turn from its great way to give
Man that must die a clearer space to live?
Why should the waters of the sea be cleft,
The hills be molten to his right and left,
That he from deep to deep might pass dry-shod,
Or look between the viewless heights on God?
Hath he such eyes as, when the shadows flee,
The sun looks out with to salute the sea?
Is his hand bounteous as the morning's hand?
Or where the night stands hath he feet to stand?
Will the storm cry not when he bids it cease?
Is it his voice that saith to the east wind, Peace?
Is his breath mightier than the west wind's breath?
Doth his heart know the things of life and death?
Can his face bring forth sunshine and give rain,
Or his weak will that dies and lives again
Make one thing certain or bind one thing fast,
That as he willed it shall be at the last?
How should the storms of heaven and kindled lights
And all the depths of things and topless heights
And air and earth and fire and water change
Their likeness, and the natural world grow strange,
And all the limits of their life undone
Lose count of time and conscience of the sun,
And that fall under which was fixed above,
That man might have a larger hour for love?"

So musing with close lips and lifted eyes
That smiled with self-contempt to live so wise,
With silent heart so hungry now so long,
So late grown clear, so miserably made strong,
About the wolds a banished man he went,
The brown wolds bare and sad as banishment,
By wastes of fruitless flowerage, and grey downs
That felt the sea-wind shake their wild-flower crowns
As through fierce hands would pluck from some grey head
The spoils of majesty despised and dead,
And fill with crying and comfortless strange sound
Their hollow sides and heights of herbless ground.
Yet as he went fresh courage on him came,

Till dawn rose too within him as a flame;
The heart of the ancient hills and his were one;
The winds took counsel with him, and the sun
Spake comfort; in his ears the shout of birds
Was as the sound of clear sweet-spirited words,
The noise of streams as laughter from above
Of the old wild lands, and as a cry of love
Spring's trumpet-blast blown over moor and lea:
The skies were red as love is, and the sea
Was as the floor of heaven for love to tread.
So went he as with light about his head,
And in the joyous travail of the year
Grew April-hearted; since nor grief nor fear
Can master so a young man's blood so long
That it shall move not to the mounting song
Of that sweet hour when earth replumes her wings
And with fair face and heart set heavenward sings
As an awakened angel unaware
That feels his sleep fall from him, and his hair
By some new breath of wind and music stirred,
Till like the sole song of one heavenly bird
Sounds all the singing of the host of heaven,
And all the glories of the sovereign Seven
Are as one face of one incorporate light.
And as that host of singers in God's sight
Might draw toward one that slumbered, and arouse
The lips requickened and rekindling brows,
So seemed the earthly host of all things born
In sight of spring and eyeshot of the morn,
All births of land or waifs of wind and sea,
To draw toward him that sorrowed, and set free
From presage and remembrance of all pains
That life that leapt and lightened in his veins.
So with no sense abashed nor sunless look,
But with exalted eyes and heart, he took
His part of sun or storm-wind, and was glad,
For all things lost, of these good things he had.

And the spring loved him surely, being from his birth
One made out of the better part of earth,
A man born as at sunrise; one that saw
Not without reverence and sweet sense of awe
But wholly without fear or fitful breath
The face of life watched by the face of death;
And living took his fill of rest and strife,
Of love and change, and fruit and seed of life,
And when his time to live in light was done
With unbent head would pass out of the sun:

A spirit as morning, fair and clear and strong,
Whose thought and work were as one harp and song
Heard through the world as in a strange king's hall
Some great guest's voice that sings of festival.
So seemed all things to love him, and his heart
In all their joy of life to take such part,
That with the live earth and the living sea
He was as one that communed mutually
With naked heart to heart of friend to friend:
And the star deepening at the sunset's end,
And the moon fallen before the gate of day
As one sore wearied with vain length of way,
And the winds wandering, and the streams and skies,
As faces of his fellows in his eyes.
Nor lacked there love where he was evermore
Of man and woman, friend of sea or shore,
Not measurable with weight of graven gold,
Free as the sun's gift of the world to hold
Given each day back to man's reconquering sight
That loses but its lordship for a night.
And now that after many a season spent
In barren ways and works of banishment,
Toil of strange fights and many a fruitless field,
Ventures of quest and vigils under shield,
He came back to the strait of sundering sea
That parts green Cornwall from grey Brittany,
Where dwelt the high king's daughter of the lands,
Iseult, named alway from her fair white hands,
She looked on him and loved him; but being young
Make shamefastness a seal upon her tongue,
And on her heart, that none might hear its cry,
Set the sweet signet of humility.
Yet when he came a stranger in her sight,
A banished man and weary, no such knight
As when the Swallow dipped her bows in foam
Steered singing that imperial Iseult home,
This maiden with her sinless sixteen years
Full of sweet thoughts and hopes that played at fears
Cast her eyes on him but in courteous wise,
And lo, the man's face burned upon her eyes
As though she had turned them on the naked sun:
And through her limbs she felt sweet passion run
As fire that flowed down from her face, and beat
Soft through stirred veins on even to her hands and feet
As all her body were one heart on flame,
Athrob with love and wonder and sweet shame.
And when he spake there sounded in her ears
As 'twere a song out of the graves of years

Heard, and again forgotten, and again
Remembered with a rapturous pulse of pain.
But as the maiden mountain snow sublime
Takes the first sense of April's trembling time
Soft on a brow that burns not though it blush
To feel the sunrise hardly half aflush,
So took her soul the sense of change, nor thought
That more than maiden love was more than nought.
Her eyes went hardly after him, her cheek
Grew scarce a goodlier flower to hear him speak,
Her bright mouth no more trembled than a rose
May for the least wind's breathless sake that blows
Too soft to sue save for a sister's kiss,
And if she sighed in sleep she knew not this.
Yet in her heart hovered the thoughts of things
Past, that with lighter or with heavier wings
Beat round about her memory, till it burned
With grief that brightened and with hope that yearned,
Seeing him so great and sad, not knowing what fate
Had bowed and crowned a head so sad and great.
Nor might she guess but little, first or last,
Though all her heart so hung upon his past,
Of what she bowed him for what sorrow's sake:
For scarce of aught at any time he spake
That from his own land oversea had sent
His lordly life to barren banishment.
Yet still or soft or keen remembrance clung
Close round her of the least word from his tongue
That fell by chance of courtesy, to greet
With grace of tender thanks to her pity, sweet
As running straems to men's way-wearied feet.
And when between strange words her name would fall,
Suddenly straightway to that lure's recall
Back would his heart bound as the falconer's bird,
And tremble and bow down before the word.
"Iseult"—and all the cloudlike world grew flame,
And all his heart flashed lightning at her name;
"Iseult"—and all the wan waste weary skies
Shone as his queen's own love-enkindled eyes.
And seeing the bright blood in his face leap up
As red wine mantling in a royal cup
To hear the sudden sweetness of the sound
Ring, but ere well his heart had time to bound
His cheek would change, and grief bowed down his head,
"Haply," the girl's heart, though she spake not, said,
"This name of mine was worn of one long dead,
Some sister that he loved: "and therewithal
Would pity bring her heart more deep in thrall.

But once, when winds about the world made mirth,
And March held revel hard on April's birth
Till air and sea were jubilant as earth,
Delight and doubt in sense and soul began,
And yearning of the maiden toward the man,
Harping on high before her: for his word
Was fire that kindled in her heart that heard,
And alway through the rhymes reverberate came
The virginal soft burden of her name.
And ere the full song failed upon her ear
Joy strove within her till it cast out fear,
And all her heart was as his harp, and rang
Swift music, made of hope whose birthnote sprang
Bright in the blood that kindled as he sang.

"Stars know not how we call them, nor may flowers
Know by what happy name the hovering hours
Baptize their new-born heads with dew and flame:
And Love, adored of all time as of ours,
Iseult, knew nought for ages of his name.

"With many tongues men called on him, but he
Wist not which word of all might worthiest be
To sound for ever in his ear the same,
Till heart of man might hear and soul might see,
Iseult, the radiance ringing from thy name.

"By many names men called him, as the night
By many a name calls many a starry light,
Her several sovereigns of dividual fame;
But day by one name only calls aright,
Iseult, the sun that bids men praise his name.

"In many a name of man his name soared high
And song shone round it soaring, till the sky
Rang rapture, and the world's fast-founded frame
Trembled with sense of triumph, even as I,
Iseult, with sense of worship at thy name.

"In many a name of woman smiled his power
Incarnate, as all summer in a flower,
Till winter bring forgetfulness or shame:
But thine, the keystone of his topless tower,
Iseult, is one with Love's own lordliest name.

"Iseult my love, Iseult my queen twice crowned,
In thee my death, in thee my life lies bound:
Names are there yet that all men's hearts acclaim,

But Love's own heart rings answer to the sound,
Iseult, that bids it bow before thy name."

There ceased his voice yearning upon the word
Struck with strong passion dumb: but she that heard
Quailed to the heart, and trembled ere her eyes
Durst let the loving light within them rise,
And yearn on his for answer: yet at last,
Albeit not all her fear was overpast,
Hope, kindling even the frost of fear apace
With sweet fleet bloom and breath of gradual grace,
Flushed in the changing roses of her face.
And ere the strife took truce of white with red,
Or joy for soft shame's sake durst lift up head,
Something she would and would not fain have said,
And wist not what the fluttering word would be,
But rose and reached forth to him her hand: and he,
Heart-stricken, bowed his head and dropped his knee,
And on her fragrant hand his lips were fire;
And their two hearts were as one trembling lyre
Touched by the keen wind's kiss with brief desire
And music shuddering at its own delight.
So dawned the moonrise of their marriage night.

IV

THE MAIDEN MARRIAGE

Spring watched her last moon burn and fade with May
While the days deepened toward a bridal day.
And on her snowbright hand the ring was set
While in the maiden's ear the song's word yet
Hovered, that hailed as love's own queen by name
Iseult: and in her heart the word was flame;
A pulse of light, a breath of tender fire,
Too dear for doubt, too driftless for desire.
Between her father's hand and brother's led
From hall to shrine, from shrine to marriage-bed,
She saw not how by hap at home-coming
Fell from her new lord's hand a royal ring,
Whereon he looked, and felt the pulse astart
Speak passion in his faith-forsaken heart.
For this was given him of the hand wherein
That heart's pledge lay for ever: so the sin
That should be done if truly he should take
This maid to wife for strange love's faithless sake

Struck all his mounting spirit abashed, and fear
Fell cold for shame's sake on his changing cheer.
Yea, shame's own fire that burned upon his brow
To bear the brand there of a broken vow
Was frozen again for very fear thereof
That wrung his heart with keener pangs than love
And all things rose upon him, all things past
Ere last they parted, cloven in twain at last,
Iseult from Tristram, Tristram from the queen;
And how men found them in the wild woods green
Sleeping, but sundered by the sword between,
Dividing breach from amorous breasts a span,
But scarce in heart the woman from the man
As far as hope from joy or sleep from truth,
And Mark that saw them held for sacred sooth
These were no fleshly lovers, by that sign
That severed them, still slumbering; so divine
He deemed it: how at waking they beheld
The king's folk round the king, and uncompelled
Were fain to follow and fare among them home
Back to the towers washed round with rolling foam
And storied halls wherethrough sea-music rang:
And how report thereafter swelled and sprang,
A full-mouthed serpent, hissing in men's ears
Word of their loves: and one of all his peers
That most he trusted, being his kinsman born,
A man base-moulded for the stamp of scorn,
Whose heart with hate was keen and cold and dark,
Gave note by midnight whisper to King Mark
Where he might take them sleeping; how ere day
Had seen the grim next morning all away
Fast bound they brought him down a weary way
With forty knights about him, and their chief
That traitor who for trust had given him grief,
To the old hoar chapel, like a strait stone tomb
Sheer on the sea-rocks, there to take his doom:
How, seeing he needs must die, he bade them yet
Bethink them if they dourest for shame forget
What deeds for Cornwall had he done, and wrought
For all their sake what rescue, when he fought
Against the fierce foul Irish foe that came
To take of them for tribute in their shame
Three hundred heads of children; whom in fight
His hand redeeming slew Moraunt the knight
That none durst lift his eyes against, not one
Had heart but he, who now had help of none,
To take the battle; whence great shame it were
To knighthood, yea, foul shame on all men there,

To see him die so shamefully: nor dourest
One man look up, nor one make answer first,
Savanna even the very traitor, who defied
And would have slain him naked in his pride,
But he, that saw the sword plucked forth to slay,
Looked on his hands, and wrenched their bonds away,
Hailing those twain that he went bound between
Suddenly to him, and kindling in his mien
Shone lion-fashion forth with eyes alight,
And lion-wise leapt on that kinsman knight
And wrung forth of his felon hands with might
The sword that should have slain him weaponless,
And smote him sheer down: then came all the press
All raging in upon him; but he wrought
So well for his deliverance as they fought
That ten strong knights rejoicingly he slew
And took no wound, nor wearied: then the crew
Waxed greater, and their cry on him; but he
Had won the chapel now above the sea
That chafed right under: then the heart in him
Sprang, seeing the low cliff clear to leap, and swim
Right out by the old blithe way the sea-mew takes
Across the bounding billow-belt that breaks
For ever, but the loud bright chain it makes
To bind the bridal bosom of the land
Time shall unlink not ever, till his hand
Fall by its own last blow dead: thence again
Might he win forth into the green great main
Far on beyond, and there yield up his breath
At least, with God's will, by no shameful death,
Or haply save himself, and come anew
Some long day later, ere sweet life were through.
And as the sea-gull hovers high, and turns
With eyes wherein the keen heart glittering yearns
Down toward the sweet green sea whereon the broad noon burns,
And suddenly, soul-stricken with delight,
Drops, and the glad wave gladdens, and the light
Sees wing and wave confuse their fluttering white,
So Tristram one brief breathing-space apart
Hung, and gazed down; then with exulting heart
Plunged: and the fleet foam round a joyous head
Flashed, that shot under, and ere a shaft had sped
Rose again radiant, a rejoicing star,
And high along the water-ways afar
Triumphed: and all they deemed he needs must die;
But Gouvernayle his squire, that watched hard by,
Sought where perchance a man might win ashore,
Striving, with strong limbs labouring long and sore,

And there abode an hour: till as from fight
Crowned with hard conquest won by mastering might.
Hardly, but happier for the imperious toil,
Swam the knight in forth of the close waves' coil,
Sea-satiate, bruised with buffets of the brine,
Laughing, and flushed as one afire with wine:
All this came hard upon him in a breath;
And how he marvelled in his heart that death
Should be no bitterer than it seemed to be
There, in the strenuous impulse of the sea
Borne as to battle deathward: and at last
How all his after seasons overpast
Had brought him darkling to this dark sweet hour,
Where his foot faltered nigh the bridal bower.
And harder seemed the passage now to pass,
Though smoother-seeming than the still sea's glass,
More fit for very manhood's heart to fear,
Than all straits past of peril. Hardly here
Might aught of all things hearten him save one,
Faith: and as men's eyes quail before the sun
So quailed his heart before the star whose light
Put out the torches of his bridal night,
So quailed and shrank with sense of faith's keen star
That burned as fire beheld by night afar
Deep in the darkness of his dreams; for all
The bride-house now seemed hung with heavier pall
Than clothes the house of mourning. Yet at last,
Soul-sick with trembling at the heart, he passed
Into the sweet light of the maiden bower
Where lay the lonely lily-featured flower
That, lying within his hand to gather, yet
Might not be gathered of it. Fierce regret
And bitter loyalty strove hard at strife
With amorous pity toward the tender wife
That wife indeed might never be, to wear
The very crown of wedlock; never bear
Children, to watch and worship her white hair
When time should change, with hand more soft than snow,
The fashion of its glory; never know
The loveliness of laughing love that lives
On little lips of children: all that gives
Glory and grace and reverence and delight
To wedded woman by her bridal right,
All praise and pride that flowers too fair to fall,
Love that should give had stripped her of them all
And left her bare for ever. So his thought
Consumed him, as a fire within that wrought
Visibly, ravening till its wrath were spent:

So pale he stood, so bowed and passion-rent,
Before the blithe-faced bride-folk, ere he went
Within the chamber, heavy-eyed: and there
Gleamed the white hands and glowed the glimmering hair
That might but move his memory more of one more fair,
More fair than all this beauty: but in sooth
So fair she too shone in her flower of youth
That scarcely might man's heart hold fast its truth,
Though strong, who gazed upon her: for her eyes
Were emerald-soft as evening-coloured skies,
And a smile in them like the light therein
Slept, or shone out in joy that knew not sin,
Clear as a child's own laughter: and her mouth,
Albeit no rose full-hearted from the south
And passion-coloured for the perfect kiss
That signs the soul for love and stamps it his,
Was soft and bright as any bud new-blown;
And through her cheek the gentler lifebloom shone
Of mild wild roses nigh the northward sea.
So in her bride-bed lay the bride: and he
Drew night, and all the high sad heart in him
Yearned on her, seeing the twilight meek and dim
Through all the soft alcove tremblingly lit
With hovering silver, as a heart in it
Beating, that burned from one deep lamp above,
Fainter than fire of torches, as the love
Within him fainter than a bridegroom's fire,
No marriage-torch red with the heart's desire,
But silver-soft, a flameless light that glowed
Starlike along night's dark and starry road
Wherein his soul was traveller. And he sighed,
Seeing, and with eyes set sadly toward his bride
Laid him down by her, and spake not: but within
His heart spake, saying how sore should be the sin
To break toward her, that of all womankind
Was faithfullest, faith plighted, or unbind
The bond first linked between them when they drank
The love-draught: and his quick blood sprang and sank,
Remembering in the pulse of all his veins
That red swift rapture, all its fiery pains
And all its fierier pleasures: and he spake
Aloud, one burning word for love's keen sake—
"Iseult;" and full of love and lovelier fear
A virgin voice gave answer—"I am here."
And a pang rent his heart at root: but still,
For spirit and flesh were vassals to his will,
Strong faith held mastery on them: and the breath
Felt on his face did not his will to death,

Nor glance nor lute-like voice nor flower-soft touch
Might so prevail upon it overmuch
That constancy might less prevail than they,
For all he looked and loved her as she lay
Smiling; and soft as bird alights on bough
He kissed her maiden mouth and blameless brow,
Once, and again his heart within him sighed:
But all his young blood's yearning toward his bride,
How hard soe'er it held his life awake
For passion, and sweet nature's unforbidden sake,
And will that strove unwillingly with will it might not break,
Fell silent as a wind abashed, whose breath
Dies out of heaven, suddenly done to death,
When in between them on the dumb dusk air
Floated the bright shade of a face more fair
Than hers that hard beside him shrank and smiled
And wist of all no more than might a child.
So had she all her heart's will, all she would,
For love's sake that sufficed her, glad and good,
All night safe sleeping in her maidenhood.

V

ISEULT AT TINTAGEL

But that same night in Cornwall oversea
Couched at Queen Iseult's hand, against her knee,
With keen kind eyes that read her whole heart's pain
Fast at wide watch lay Tristram's hound Hodain,
The goodliest and the mightiest born on earth,
That many a forest day of fiery mirth
Had plied his craft before them; and the queen
Cherished him, even for those dim years between,
More than of old in those bright months far flown
When ere a blast of Tristram's horn was blown
Each morning as the woods rekindled, ere
Day gat full empire of the glimmering air,
Delight of dawn would quicken him, and fire
Spring and pant in his breath with bright desire
To be among the dewy ways on quest:
But now perforce at restless-hearted rest
He chafed through days more barren than the sand,
Soothed hardly but soothed only with her hand,
Though fain to fawn thereon and follow, still
With all his heart and all his loving will
Desiring one divided from his sight,

For whose lost sake dawn was as dawn of night
And noon as night's noon in his eyes was dark.
But in the halls far under sat King Mark,
Feasting, and full of cheer, with heart uplift,
As on the night that harper gat his gift:
And music revelled on the fitful air,
And songs came floated up the festal stair,
And muffled roar of wassail, where the king
Took heart from wine-cups and the quiring string
Till all his cold thin veins rejoiced and ran
Strong as with lifeblood of a kinglier man.
But the queen shut from sound her wearied ears,
Shut her sad eyes from sense of aught save tears,
And wrung her hair with soft fierce hands, and prayed:
"O God, God born of woman, of a maid,
Christ, once in flesh of thine own fashion clad;
O very love, so glad in heaven and sad
On earth for earth's sake alway; since thou art
Pure only, I only impure of spirit and heart,
Since thou for sin's sake and the bitter doom
Didst as a veil put on a virgin's womb,
I that am none, and cannot hear or see
Or shadow or likeness or a sound of thee
Far off, albeit with man's own speech and face
Thou shine yet and thou speak yet, showing forth grace—
Ah me! grace only shed on souls that are
Lit and led forth of shadow by thy star—
Alas! to these men only grace, to these,
Lord, whom thy love draws Godward, to thy knees—
I, can I draw thee me-ward, can I seek,
Who love thee not, to love me? seeing how weak,
Lord, all this little love I bear thee is,
And how much is my strong love more than this,
My love that I love man with, that I bear
Him sinning through me sinning? wilt thou care,
God, for this love, if love be any, alas,
In me to give thee, though long since there was,
How long, when I too, Lord, was clean, even I,
That now am unclean till the day I die—
Haply by burning, harlot-fashion, made
A horror in all hearts of wife and maid,
Hateful, not knowing if ever in these mine eyes
Shone any light of thine in any wise
Or this were love at all that I bore thee?"

And the night spake, and thundered on the sea,
Ravening aloud for ruin of lives: and all
The bastions of the main cliff's northward wall

Rang response out from all their deepening length,
As the east wind girded up his godlike strength
And hurled in hard against that high-towered hold
The fleeces of the flock that knows no fold,
The rent white shreds of shattering storm: but she
Heard not nor heeded wind or storming sea,
Knew not if night were mild or mad with wind.

"Yea, though deep lips and tender hair be thinned,
Though cheek wither, brow fade, and bosom wane,
Shall I change also from this heart again
To maidenhood of heart and holiness?
Shall I more love thee, Lord, or love him less—
Ah miserable! though spirit and heart be rent,
Shall I repent, Lord God? shall I repent?
Nay, though thou slay me! for herein I am blest,
That as I loved him yet I love him best —
More than mine own soul or thy love or thee,
Though thy love save and my love save not me.
Blest am I beyond women ever herein,
That beyond all born women is my sin,
And perfect my transgression: that above
All offerings of all others is my love,
Who have chosen it only, and put away for this
Thee, and my soul's hope, Saviour, of the kiss
Wherewith thy lips make welcome all thine own
When in them life and death are overthrown;
The sinless lips that seal the death of sin,
The kiss wherewith their dumb lips touched begin
Singing in heaven.

"Where we shall never, love,
Never stand up nor sing! for God above
Knows us, how too much more than God to me
Thy sweet love is, my poor love is to thee!
Dear, dost thou see now, dost thou hear to-night
Sleeping, my waste wild speech, my face worn white,
—Speech once heard soft by thee, face once kissed red!—
In such a dream as when men see their dead
And know not if they know if dead these be?
Ah love, are thy days my days, and to thee
Are all nights like as my nights? does the sun
Grieve thee? art thou soul-sick till day be done,
And weary till day rises? is thine heart
Full of dead things as mine is? Nay, thou art
Man, with man's strength and praise and pride of life,
No bondwoman, no queen, no loveless wife
That would be shamed albeit she had not sinned."

And swordlike was the sound of the iron wind,
And as a breaking battle was the sea.

"Nay, Lord, I pray thee let him love not me,
Love me not any more, nor like me die,
And be no more than such a thing as I.
Turn his heart from me, lest my love too lose
Thee as I lose thee, and his fair soul refuse
For my sake thy fair heaven, and as I fell
Fall, and be mixed with my soul and with hell.
Let me die rather, and only; let me be
Hated of him so he be loved of thee,
Lord: for I would not have him with me there
Out of thy light and love in the unlit air,
Out of thy sight in the unseen hell where I
Go gladly, going alone, so thou on high
Lift up his soul and love him—Ah, Lord, Lord,
Shalt thou love as I love him? she that poured
From the alabaster broken at thy feet
An ointment very precious, not so sweet
As that poured likewise forth before thee then
From the rehallowed heart of Magdalen,
From a heart broken, yearning like the dove,
An ointment very precious which is love—
Couldst thou being holy and God, and sinful she,
Love her indeed as surely she loved thee?
Nay, but if not, then as we sinners can
Let us love still in the old sad wise of man.
For with less love than my love, having had
Mine, though God love him he shall not be glad
And with such love as my love, I wot well,
She shall not lie disconsolate in hell:
Sad only as souls for utter love's sake be
Here, and a little sad, perchance, for me—
Me happy, me more glad than God above,
In the utmost hell whose fires consume not love!
For in the waste ways emptied of the sun
He would say—'Dear, thy place is void, and one
Weeps among angels for thee, with his face
Veiled, saying, O sister, how thy chosen place
Stands desolate, that God made fair for thee!
Is heaven not sweeter, and we thy brethren, we
Fairer than love on earth and life in hell?'
And I—with me were all things then not well?
Should I not answer—'O love, be well content;
Look on me, and behold if I repent.'
This were more to me than an angel's wings.

Yea, many men pray God for many things,
But I pray that this only thing may be."

And as a full field charging was the sea,
And as the cry of slain men was the wind.

"Yea, since I surely loved him, and he sinned
Surely, though not as my sin his be black,
God, give him to me—God, God, give him back!
For now how should we live in twain or die?
I am he indeed, thou knowest, and he is I.
Not man and woman several as we were,
But one thing with one life and death to bear.
How should one love his own soul overmuch?
And time is long since last I felt the touch,
The sweet touch of my lover, hand and breath,
In such delight as puts delight to death,
Burn my soul through, till the spirit and soul and sense,
In the sharp grasp of the hour, with violence
Died, and again through pangs of violent birth
Lived, and laughed out with refluent might of mirth;
Laughed each on other and shuddered into one,
As a cloud shuddering dies into the sun.
Ah, sense is that or spirit, soul or flesh,
That only love lulls or awakes afresh?
Ah, sweet is that or bitter, evil or good,
That very love allays not as he would?
Nay, truth is this or vanity, that gives
No love assurance when love dies or lives?
This that my spirit is wrung withal, and yet
No surelier knows if haply thine forget,
Thou that my spirit is wrung for, nor can say
Love is not in thee dead as yesterday?
Dost thou feel, thou, this heartbeat whence my heart
Would send thee word what life is mine apart,
And know by keen response what life is thine?
Dost thou not hear one cry of all of mine?
O Tristram's heart, have I no part in thee?"

And all her soul was as the breaking sea,
And all her heart anhungered as the wind.

"Dost thou repent thee of the sin we sinned?
Dost thou repent thee of the days and nights
That kindled and that quenched for us their lights,
The months that feasted us with all their hours,
The ways that breathed of us in all their flowers,
The dells that sang of us with all their doves?

Dost thou repent thee of the wildwood loves?
Is thine heart chanted, and hallowed? art thou grown
God's, and not mine? Yet, though my heart make moan,
Fain would my soul give thanks for thine, if thou
Be saved — yea, fain praise God, and knows not how.
How should it know thanksgiving? nay, or learn
Aught of the love wherewith thine own should burn,
God's that should cast out as an evil thing
Mine? yea, what hand or prayer have I to cling,
What heart to prophesy, what spirit of sight
To strain insensual eyes towards increate light,
Who look but back on life wherein I sinned?"

And all their past came wailing in the wind,
And all their future thundered in the sea.

"But if my soul might touch the time to be,
If hand might handle now or eye behold
My life and death ordained me from of old,
Life palpable, compact of blood and breath,
Visible, present, naked, very death,
Should I desire to know before the day
These that I know not, nor is man that may?
For haply, seeing, my heart would break for fear,
And my soul timeless cast its load off here,
Its load of life too bitter, love too sweet,
And fall down shamed and naked at thy feet,
God, who wouldst take no pity of it, nor give
One hour back, one of all its hours to live
Clothed with my mortal body, that once more,
Once, on this reach of barren beaten shore,
This stormy strand of life, ere sail were set,
Had haply felt love's arms about it yet—
Yea, ere death's bark put off to seaward, might
With many a grief have bought me one delight
That then should know me never. Ah, what years
Would I endure not, filled up full with tears,
Bitter like blood and dark as dread of death,
To win one amorous hour of mingling breath,
One fire-eyed hour and sunnier than the sun,
For all these days and nights like nights but one?
One hour of heaven born once, a stormless birth,
For all these windy, weary hours of earth?
One, but one hour from birth of joy to death,
For all these hungering hours of feverish breath?
And I should lose this, having died and sinned."

And as a man's anguish clamouring cried the wind,

And as God's anger answering rang the sea.

"And yet what life—Lord God, what life for me
Has thy strong wrath made ready? Dost thou think
How lips whose thirst hath only tears to drink
Grow grey for grief untimely? Dost thou know,
O happy God, how men wax weary of woe—
Yea, for their wrong's sake that thine hand hath done
Come even to hate thy semblance in the sun?
Turn back from dawn and noon and all thy light
To make their souls one with the soul of night?
Christ, if thou hear yet or have eyes to see,
Thou that hadst pity, and hast no pity on me,
Know'st thou no more, as in this life's sharp span,
What pain thou hadst on earth, what pain hath man?
Hast thou no care, that all we suffer yet?
What help is ours of thee if thou forget?
What profit have we though thy blood were given,
Not love but hate, thou bitter God and strange,
Whose heart as man's heart hath grown cold with change,
Not love but hate thou showest us that have sinned."

And like a world's cry shuddering was the wind,
And like a God's voice threatening was the sea.

"Nay, Lord, for thou wast gracious; nay, in thee
No change can come with time or varying fate,
No tongue bid thine be less compassionate,
No sterner eye rebuke for mercy thine,
No sin put out thy pity — no, not mine.
Thou knowest us, Lord, thou knowest us, all we are,
He, and the soul that hath his soul for star:
Thou knowest as I know, Lord how much more worth
Than all souls clad and clasped about with earth,
But most of all, God, how much more than I,
Is this man's soul that surely shall not die.
What righteousness, what judgment, Lord most high,
Were this, to bend a brow of doom as grim
As threats me, the adulterous wife, on him?
There lies none other nightly by his side:
He hath not sought, he shall not seek a bride.
For as God sunders earth from heaven above,
So far was my love born beneath his love.
I loved him as the sea-wind loves the sea,
To rend and ruin it only and waste: but he,
As the sea loves a sea-bird loved he me,
To foster and uphold my tired life's wing,
And bounteously beneath me spread forth spring,

A springtide space whereon to float or fly,
A world of happy water, whence the sky
Glowed goodlier, lightening from so glad a glass,
Than with its own light only. Now, alas!
Cloud hath come down and clothed it round with storm,
And gusts and fits of eddying winds deform
The feature of its glory. Yet be thou,
God, merciful: nay, show but justice now,
And let the sin in him that scarce was his
Stand expiated with exile: and be this
The price for him, the atonement this, that I
With all the sin upon me live, and die
With all thy wrath on me that most have sinned."
And like man's heart relenting sighted the wind,
And as God's wrath subsiding sank the sea.

"But if such grace be possible—if it be
Not sin more strange than all sins past, and worse
Evil, that cries upon thee for a curse,
To pray such prayers from such a heart, do thou
Hear, and make wide thine hearing toward me now;
Let not my soul and his for ever dwell
Sundered: though doom keep always heaven and hell
Irreconcilable, infinitely apart,
Keep not in twain for ever heart and heart
That once, albeit by not thy law, were one;
Let this be not thy will, that this be done.
Let all else, all thou wilt of evil, be,
But no doom, none, dividing him and me."

By this was heaven stirred eastward, and there came
Up the rough ripple a labouring light like flame;
And dawn, sore trembling still and grey with fear,
Looked hardly forth, a face of heavier cheer
Than one which grief or dread yet half enshrouds,
Wild-eyed and wan, across the cleaving clouds.
And Iseult, worn with watch long held on pain.
Turned, and her eye lit on the hound Hodain,
And all her heart went out in tears: and he
Laid his kind head along her bended knee,
Till round his neck her arms went hard, and all
The night past from her as a chain might fall:
But yet the heart within her, half undone,
Wailed, and was loth to let her see the sun.

And ere full day brought heaven and earth to flower,
Far thence, a maiden in a marriage bower,
That moment, hard by Tristram, oversea,

Woke with glad eyes Iseult of Brittany.

VI

JOYOUS GARD

A little time, O Love, a little light,
A little hour for ease before the night.
Sweet Love, that art so bitter; foolish Love,
Whom wise men know for wiser, and thy dove
More subtle than the serpent; for thy sake
These pray thee for a little beam to break,
A little grace to help them, lest men think
Thy servants have but hours like tears to drink.
O Love, a little comfort, lest they fear
To serve as these have served thee who stand here.

For these are thine, thy servants these, that stand
Here nigh the limit of the wild north land,
At margin of the grey great eastern sea,
Dense-islanded with peaks and reefs, that see
No life but of the fleet wings fair and free
Which cleave the mist and sunlight all day long
With sleepless flight and cries more glad than song.
Strange ways of life have led them hither, here
To win fleet respite from desire and fear
With armistice from sorrow; strange and sweet
Ways trodden by forlorn and casual feet
Till kindlier chance woke toward them kindly will
In happier hearts of lovers, and their ill
Found rest, as healing surely might it not,
By gift and kingly grace of Launcelot
At gracious bidden given of Guenevere.
For in the trembling twilight of this year
Ere April spring from hope to certitude
Two hearts of friends fast linked had fallen at feud
As they rode forth on hawking, by the sign
Which gave his new bride's brother Ganhardine
To know the truth of Tristram's dealing, how
Faith kept of him against his marriage vow
Kept virginal his bride-bed night and morn;
Whereat, as wroth his blood should suffer scorn,
Came Ganhardine to Tristram, saying, "Behold,
We have loved thee, and for love we have shown of old
Scorn hast thou shown us: wherefore is thy bride
Not thine indeed, a stranger at thy side,

Contemned? what evil hath she done, to be
Mocked with mouth-marriage and despised of thee,
Shamed, set at nought, rejected?" But there came
On Tristram's brow and eye the shadow and flame
Confused of wrath and wonder, ere he spake,
Saying, "Hath she bid thee for thy sister's sake
Plead with me, who believed of her in heart
More nobly than to deem such piteous part
Should find so fair a player? or whence has thou
Of us this knowledge?" "Nay," said he, "but now,
Riding beneath these whitethorns overhead,
There fell a flower into her girdlestead
Which laughing she shook out, and smiling said —
'Lo, what large leave the wind hath given this stray,
To lie more near my heart than till this day
Aught ever since my mother lulled me lay
Or even my lord came ever;' whence I wot
We are all thy scorn, a race regarded not
Nor held as worth communion of thine own,
Except in her be found some fault alone
To blemish our alliance." Then replied
Tristram, "Nor blame nor scorn may touch my bride,
Albeit unknown of love she live, and be
Worth a man worthier than her love thought me.
Faith only, faith withheld me, faith forbade
The blameless grace wherewith love's grace makes glad
All lives linked else in wedlock; not that less
I loved the sweet light of her loveliness,
But that my love toward faith was more: and thou
Albeit thine heart be keen against me now,
Couldst thou behold my very lady, then
No more of thee than of all other men
Should this my faith be held a faithless fault."
And ere that day their hawking came to halt,
Being sore of him entreated for a sign,
He swore to bring his brother Ganhardine
To sight of that strange Iseult: and thereon
Forth soon for Carwall are these brethren gone,
Even to that royal pleasance where the hunt
Rang ever of old with Tristram's horn in front
Blithe as the queen's horse bounded at his side:
And first of all her dames forth pranced in pride
That day before them, with a ringing rein
All golden-glad, the king's false bride Brangwain,
The queen's true handmaid ever: and on her
Glancing, "Be called for all time truth-teller,
O Tristram, of all true men's tongues alive,"
Quoth Ganhardine; "for may my soul so thrive

As yet mine eye drank never sight like this."
"Ay?" Tristram said, "and she thou look'st on is
So great in grace of goodliness, that thou
Hast less thought left of wrath against me now,
Seeing but my lady's handmaid? Nay, behold;
See'st thou no light more golden than of gold
Shine where she moves in midst of all, above
All, past all price or praise or prayer of love?
Lo, this is she." But as one mazed with wine
Stood, stunned in spirit and stricken, Ganhardine,
And gazed out hard against them: and his heart
As with a sword was cloven, and rent apart
As with strong fangs of fire; and scarce he spake,
Saying how his life for even a handmaid's sake
Was made a flame within him. And the knight
Bade him, being known of none that stood in sight,
Bear to Brangwain his ring, that she unseen
Might give in token privily to the queen
And send swift word where under moon or sun
They twain might yet be no more twain but one.
And that same night, under the stars that rolled
Over their warm deep wildwood nights of old
Whose hours for grains of sand shed sparks of fire,
Such was made anew for their desire
By secret wile of sickness feigned, to keep
The king far off her vigils or her sleep,
That in the queen's pavilion midway set
By glimmering moondawn were those lovers met,
And Ganhardine of Brangwain gat him grace.
And in some passionate soft interspace
Between two swells of passion, when their lips
Breathed, and made room for such brief speech as slips
From tongues athirst with draughts of amorous wine
That leaves them thirstier than the salt sea's brine,
Was counsel taken how to fly, and where
Find covert from the wild word's ravening air
That hunts with storm the feet of nights and days
Through strange thwart lines of life and flowerless ways.
Then said Iseult: "Lo, now the chance is here
Foreshown me late by word of Guenevere,
To give me comfort of thy rumoured wrong,
My traitor Tristram, when report was strong
Of me forsaken and thine heart estranged:
Nor should her sweet soul toward me yet be changed
Nor all her love lie barren, if mine hand
Crave harvest of it from the flowering land.
See therefore if this counsel please thee not,
That we take horse in haste for Camelot

And seek that friendship of her plighted troth
Which love shall be full fain to lend, nor loth
Shall my love be to take it." So next night
The multitudinous stars laughed round their flight,
Fulfilling far with laughter made of light
The encircling deeps of heaven: and in brief space
At Camelot their long love gat them grace
Of those fair twain whose heads men's praise impearled
As love's two lordliest lovers in the world:
And thence as guests for harbourage past they forth
To win this noblest hold of all the north.
Far by wild ways and many days they rode,
Till clear across June's kingliest sunset glowed
The great round girth of goodly wall that showed
Where for one clear sweet season's length should be
Their place of strength to rest in, fain and free,
By the utmost margin of the loud lone sea.

And now, O Love, what comfort? God most high,
Whose life is as a flower's to live and die,
Whose light is everlasting: Lord, whose breath
Speaks music through the deathless lips of death
Whereto time's heart rings answer: Bard, whom time
Hears, and is vanquished with a wandering rhyme
That once thy lips made fragrant: Seer, whose sooth
Joy knows not well, but sorrow knows for truth,
Being priestess of thy soothsayings: Love, what grace
Shall these twain find at last before thy face?

This many a year they have served thee, and deserved,
If ever man might yet of all that served,
Since the first heartbeat bade the first man's knee
Bend, and his mouth take music, praising thee,
Some comfort; and some honey indeed of thine
Thou hast mixed for these with life's most bitter wine,
Commending to their passionate lips a draught
No deadlier than thy chosen of old have quaffed
And blessed thine hand, their cupbearer's: for not
On all men comes the grace that seals their lot
As holier in thy sight, for all these feuds
That rend it, than the light-souled multitude's,
Nor thwarted of thine hand nor blessed; but these
Shall see no twilight, Love, nor fade at ease,
Grey-grown and careless of desired delight,
But lie down tired and sleep before the night.
These shall not live till time or change may chill
Or doubt divide or shame subdue their will,
Or fear or slow repentance work them wrong,

Or love die first: these shall not live so long.
Death shall not take them drained of dear true life
Already, sick or stagnant from the strife,
Quenched: not with dry-drawn veins and lingering breath
Shall these through crumbling hours crouch down to death.
Swift, with one strong clean leap, ere life's pulse tire,
Most like the leap of lions or of fire,
Sheer death shall bound upon them: one pang past,
The first keen sense of him shall be their last,
Their last shall be no sense of any fear,
More than their life had sense of anguish here.

Weeks and light months had fled at swallow's speed
Since here their first hour sowed for them the seed
Of many sweet as rest or hope could be;
Since on the blown beach of a glad new sea
Wherein strange rocks like fighting men stand scarred
They saw the strength and help of Joyous Gard.
Within the full deep glorious tower that stands
Between the wild sea and the broad wild lands
Love led and gave them quiet: and they drew
Life like a God's life in each wind that blew,
And took their rest, and triumphed. Day by day
The mighty moorlands and the sea-walls grey,
The brown bright waters of green fells that sing
One song to rocks and flowers and birds on wing,
Beheld the joy and glory that they had,
Passing, and how the whole world made them glad,
And their great love was mixed with all things great,
As life being lovely, and yet being strong like fate.
For when the sun sprang on the sudden sea
Their eyes sprang eastward, and the day to be
Was lit in them untimely: such delight
They took yet of the clear cold breath and light
That goes before the morning, and such grace
Was deathless in them through their whole life's space
As dies in many with their dawn that dies
And leaves in pulseless hearts and flameless eyes
No light to lighten and no tear to weep
For youth's high joy that time has cast on sleep.
Yea, this old grace and height of joy they had,
To lose no jot of all that made them glad
And filled their springs of spirit with such fire
That all delight fed in them all desire;
And no whit less than in their first keen prime
The spring's breath blew through all their summer time,
And in their skies would sunlike Love confuse
Clear April colours with hot August hues,

And in their hearts one light of sun and moon
Reigned, and the morning died not of the noon:
Such might of life was in them, and so high
Their heart of love rose higher than fate could fly.
And many a large delight of hawk and hound
The great glad land that knows no bourne or bound,
Save the wind's own and the outer sea-bank's, gave
Their days for comfort; many a long blithe wave
Buoyed their blithe bark between the bare bald rocks,
Deep, steep, and still, save for the swift free flocks
Unshepherded, uncompassed, unconfined,
That when blown foam keeps all the loud air blind
Mix with the wind's their triumph, and partake
The joy of blasts that ravin, waves that break,
All round and all below their mustering wings,
A clanging cloud that round the cliff's edge clings
On each bleak bluff breaking the strenuous tides
That rings reverberate mirth when the storm bestrides
The subject night in thunder: many a noon
They took the moorland's or the bright sea's boon
With all their hearts into their spirit of sense,
Rejoicing, where the sudden dells grew dense
With sharp thick flight of hillside birds, or where
On some strait rock's ledge in the intense mute air
Erect against the cliff's sheer sunlit white
Blue as the clear north heaven, clothed warm with light,
Stood neck to bended neck and wing to wing
With heads fast hidden under, close as cling
Flowers on one flowering almond-branch in spring
Three herons deep asleep against the sun,
Each with one bright foot downward poised, and one
Wing-hidden hard by the bright head, and all
Still as fair shapes fixed on some wondrous wall
Of minister-aisle or cloister-close or hall
To take even time's eye prisoner with delight.
Or, satisfied with joy of sound and sight,
They sat and communed of things past: what state
King Arthur, yet unwarred upon by fate,
Held high in hall at Camelot, like one
Whose lordly life was as the mounting sun
That climbs and pauses on the point of noon,
Sovereign: how royal rang the tourney's tune
Through Tristram's three days' triumph, spear to spear,
When Iseult shone enthroned by Guenevere,
Rose against rose, the highest adored on earth,
Imperial: yet with subtle notes of mirth
Would she bemock her praises, and bemoan
Her glory by that splendour overthrown

Which lightened from her sister's eyes elate;
Saying how by night a little light seems great,
But less than least of all things, very nought,
When dawn undoes the web that darkness wrought;
How like a tower of ivory well designed
By subtlest hand subserving subtlest mind,
Ivory with flower of rose incarnadined
And kindling with some God therein revealed,
A light for grief to look on and be healed,
Stood Guenevere: and all beholding her
Were heartstruck even as earth at midsummer
With burning wonder, hardly to be borne.
So was that amorous glorious lady born,
A fiery memory for all storied years:
Nor might men call her sisters crowned her peers,
Her sister queens, put all by her to scorn:
She had such eyes as are not made to mourn;
But in her own a gleaming ghost of tears
Shone, and their glance was slower than Guenevere's,
And fitfuller with fancies grown of grief
Shamed as a Mayflower shames an autumn leaf
Full well she wist it could not choose but be
If in that other's eyeshot standing she
Should lift her looks up ever: wherewithal
Like fires whose light fills heaven with festival
Flamed her eyes full on Tristram's; and he laughed
Answering, "What wile of sweet child-hearted craft
That children forge for children, to beguile
Eyes known of them not witless of the wile
But fain to seem for sport's sake self-deceived,
Wilt thou find out now not to be believed?
Or how shall I trust more than ouphe or elf
Thy truth to me-ward, who beliest thyself?"
"Nor elf nor ouphe or aught of airier kind,"
Quoth she, "though made of moonbeams moist and blind,
Is light if weighed with man's winged weightless mind.
Though thou keep somewise troth with me, God wot,
When thou didst wed, I doubt, thou thoughtest not
So charily to keep it." "Nay," said he,
"Yet am not I rebukable by thee
As Launcelot, erring held me ere he wist
No mouth save thine of mine was ever kissed
Save as a sister's only, since we twain
Drank first the draught assigned our lips to drain
That Fate and Love with darkling hands commixt
Poured, and now power to part them came betwixt,
But either's will, howbeit they seem at strife,
Was toward us one, as death itself and life

Are one sole doom toward all men, nor may one
Behold not darkness, who beholds the sun."

"Ah, then," she said, "what word is this mean hear
Of Merlin, how some doom too strange to fear
Was cast but late about him oversea,
Sweet recreant, in thy bridal Brittany?
Is not his life sealed fast on him with sleep,
By witchcraft of his own and love's, to keep
Till earth be fire and ashes?"

"Surely," said
Her lover, "not as one alive or dead
The great good wizard, well beloved and well
Predestinate of heaven that casts out hell
For guerdon gentler far than all men's fate,
Exempt alone of all predestinate,
Takes his strange rest at heart of slumberland,
More deep asleep in green Broceliande
Than shipwrecked sleepers in the soft green sea
Beneath the weight of wandering waves: but he
Hath for those roofing waters overhead
Above him always all the summer spread
Or all the winter wailing: or the sweet
Late leaves marked red with autumn's burning feet,
Or withered with his weeping, round the seer
Rain, and he sees not, nor may heed or hear
The witness of the winter: but in spring
He hears above him all the winds on wing
Through the blue dawn between the brightening boughs,
And on shut eyes and slumber-smitten brows
Feels ambient change in the air and strengthening sun,
And knows the soul that was his soul at one
With the ardent world's, and in the spirit of earth
His sprit of life reborn to mightier birth
And mixed with things of elder life than ours;
With cries of birds, and kindling lamps of flowers,
And sweep and song of winds, and fruitful light
Of sunbeams, and the far faint breath of night,
And waves and woods at morning: and in all,
Soft as at noon the slow sea's rise and fall,
He hears in spirit a song that none but he
Hears from the mystic mouth of Nimue
Shed like a consecration; and his heart,
Hearing, is made for love's sake as a part
Of that far singing, and the life thereof
Part of that life that feeds the world with love:
Yea, heart in heart is molten, hers and his,

Into the world's heart and the soul that is
Beyond or sense or vision; and their breath
Stirs the soft springs of deathless life and death,
Death that bears life, and change that brings forth seed
Of life to death and death to life indeed,
As blood recircling through the unsounded veins
Of earth and heaven with all their joys and pains.
Ah, that when love shall laugh no more nor weep
We too, we too might hear that song and sleep!"

"Yea," said Iseult, "some joy it were to be
Lost in the sun's light and the all-girdling sea,
Mixed with the winds and woodlands, and to bear
Part in the large life of the quickening air,
And the sweet earth's, our mother: yet to pass
More fleet than mirrored faces from the glass
Out of all pain and all delight, so far
That love should seem but as the furthest star
Sunk deep in trembling heaven, scarce seen or known,
As a dead moon forgotten, once that shone
Where now the sun shines — nay, not all things yet,
Not all things always, dying would I forget."

And Tristram answered amorously, and said:
"O heart that here art mine, O heavenliest head
That ever took men's worship here, which art
Mine, how shall death put out the fire at heart,
Quench in men's eyes the head's remembered light,
That time shall set but higher in more men's sight?
Think thou not much to die one earthly day,
Being made not in their mould who pass away
Nor who shall pass for ever."

"Ah," she said,
"What shall it profit me, being praised and dead?
What profit have the flowers of all men's praise?
What pleasure of our pleasure have the days
That pour on us delight of life and mirth?
What fruit of all our joy on earth has earth?
Nor am I—nay, my lover, am I one
To take such part in heaven's enkindling sun
And in the inviolate air and sacred sea
As clothes with grace that wondrous Nimue?
For all her works are bounties, all her deeds
Blessings; her days are scrolls wherein love reads
The record of his mercies; heaven above
Hath not more heavenly holiness of love
Than earth beneath, wherever pass or pause

Her feet that move not save by love's own laws,
In gentleness of godlike wayfaring
To heal men's hearts as earth is healed by spring
Of all such woes as winter: what am I,
Love, that have strength but to desire and die,
That have but grace to love and do thee wrong,
What am I that my name should live so long,
Save as the star that crossed thy star-struck lot,
With hers whose light was life to Launcelot?
Life gave she him, and strength, and fame to be
For ever: I, what gift can I give thee?
Peril and sleepless watches, fearful breath
Of dread more bitter for my sake than death
When death came nigh to call me by my name,
Exile, rebuke, remorse, and —O, not shame.
Shame only, this I gave thee not, whom none
May give that worst thing ever — no, not one.
Of all that hate, all hateful hearts that see
Darkness for light and hate where love should be,
None for my shame's sake may speak shame of thee."

And Tristram answering ere he kissed her smiled:
"O very woman, god at once and child,
What ails thee to desire of me once more
The assurance that thou hadst in heart before?
For all this wild sweet waste of sweet vain breath,
Thou knowest I know thou has given me life, not death.
The shadow of death, informed with shows of strife,
Was ere I won thee all I had of life.
Light war, light love, light living, dreams in sleep,
Joy slight and light, not glad enough to weep,
Filled up my foolish days with sound and shine,
Vision and gleam from strange men's cast on mine,
Reverberate light from eyes presaging thine
That shed but shadowy moonlight where thy face
Now sheds forth sunshine in the deep same place,
The deep live heart half dead and shallower then
Than summer fords which thwart not wandering men.
For how should I, signed sorrow's from my birth,
Kiss dumb the loud red laughing lips of mirth?
Or how, sealed thine to be, love less than heaven on earth?
My heart in me was held at restless rest,
Presageful of some prize beyond its quest,
Prophetic still with promise, fain to find the best.
For one was fond and one was blithe and one
Fairer than all save twain whose peers are none;
For third on earth is none that heaven hath seen
To stand with Guenevere beside my queen.

Not Nimue, girt with blessing as a guard:
Not the soft lures and laughters of Ettarde:
Not she, that splendour girdled round with gloom,
Crowned as with iron darkness of the tomb,
And clothed with clouding conscience of a monstrous doom,
Whose blind incestuous love brought forth a fire
To burn her ere it burn its darkling sire,
Her mother's son, King Arthur: yet but late
We saw pass by that fair live shadow of fate,
The queen Morgause of Orkney, like a dream
That scares the night when moon and starry beam
Sicken and swoon before some sorcerer's eyes
Whose wordless charms defile the saintly skies,
Bright still with fire and pulse of blood and breath,
Whom her own sons have doomed for shame to death."

"Death—yea," quoth she, "there is not said or heard
So oft aloud on earth so sure a word.
Death, and again death, and for each that saith
Ten tongues chime answer to the sound of death.
Good end God send us ever — so men pray.
But I — this end God send me, would I say,
To die not of division and a heart
Rent or with sword of severance cloven apart,
But only when thou diest and only where thou art,
O thou my soul and spirit and breath to me,
O light, life, love! yea, let this only be,
That dying I may praise God who gave me thee,
Let hap what will thereafter."

So that day
They communed, even till even was worn away,
Nor aught they said seemed strange or sad to say,
But sweet as night's dim dawn to weariness.
Nor loved they life or love for death's sake less,
Nor feared they death for love's or life's sake more
And on the sounding soft funereal shore
They, watching till the day should wholly die,
Saw the far sea sweep to the far grey sky,
Saw the long sands sweep to the long grey sea.
And night made one sweet mist of moor and lea,
And only far off shore the foam gave light.
And life in them sank silent as the night.

VII

THE WIFE'S VIGIL

But all that year in Brittany forlorn,
More sick at heart with wrath than fear of scorn
And less in love with love than grief, and less
With grief than pride of spirit and bitterness,
Till all the sweet life of her blood was changed
And all her soul from all her past estranged
And all her will with all itself at strife
And all her mind at war with all her life,
Dwelt the white-handed Iseult, maid and wife,
A mourner that for mourning robes had on
Anger and doubt and hate of things foregone.
For that sweet spirit of old which made her sweet
Was parched with blasts of thought as flowers with heat
And withered as with wind of evil will;
Though slower than frosts or fires consume or kill
That bleak black wind vexed all her spirit still.
As ripples reddening in the roughening breath
Of the eager east when dawn does night to death,
So rose and stirred and kindled in her thought
Fierce barren fluctuant fires that lit not aught,
But scorched her soul with yearning keen as hate
And dreams that left her wrath disconsolate.
When change came first on that first heaven where all
Life's hours were flowers that dawn's light hand let fall,
The sun that smote her dewy cloud of days
Wrought from its showery folds his rainbow's rays,
For love the red, for hope the gentle green,
But yellow jealously glared pale between.
Ere yet the sky grew heavier, and her head
Bent flowerwise, chill with change and fancies fled,
She saw but love arch all her heaven across with red,
A burning bloom that seemed to breathe and beat
And waver only as flame with rapturous heat
Wavers; and all the world therewith smelt sweet,
As incense kindling from the rose-red flame:
And when that full flush waned, and love became
Scarce fainter, though his fading horoscope
From certitude of sight receded, hope
Held yet her April-coloured light aloft
As though to lure back love, a lamp sublime and soft.
But soon that light paled as a leaf grows pale
And fluttered leaf-like in the gathering gale
And melted even as dew-flakes, whose brief sheen
The sun that gave despoils of glittering green;
Till harder shone 'twixt hope and love grown cold
A sallow light like withering autumn's gold,

The pale strong flame of jealous thought, that glows
More deep than hope's green bloom or love's enkindled rose:
As though the sunflower's faint fierce disk absorbed
The spirit and heart of starrier flowers disorbed.

That same full hour of twilight's doors unbarred
To let bright night behold in Joyous Gard
The glad grave eyes of lovers far away
Watch with sweet thoughts of death the death of day
Saw lonelier by the narrower opening sea
Sit fixed at watch Iseult of Brittany.
As darkness from deep valleys void and bleak
Climbs till it clothe with night the sunniest peak
Where only of all a mystic mountain-land
Day seems to cling yet with a trembling hand
And yielding heart reluctant to recede,
So, till her soul was clothed with night indeed,
Rose the slow cloud of envious will within
And hardening hate that held itself no sin,
Veiled heads of vision, eyes of evil gleam,
Dim thought on thought, and darkling dream on dream.
Far off she saw in spirit, and seeing abhorred,
The likeness wrought on darkness of her lord
Shine, and the imperial semblance at his side
Whose shadow from her seat cast down the bride,
Whose power and ghostly presence thrust her forth:
Beside that unknown other sea far north
She saw them, clearer than in present sight
Rose on her eyes the starry shadow of night;
And on her heart that heaved with gathering fate
Rose red with storm the starless shadow of hate;
And eyes and heart made one saw surge and swell
The fires of sunset like the fires of hell.
As though God's wrath would burn up sin with shame,
The incensed red gold of deepening heaven grew flame:
The sweet green spaces of the soft low sky
Faded, as fields that withering wind leaves dry:
The sea's was like a doomsman's blasting breath
From lips afoam with ravenous lust of death.
A night like desolation, sombre-starred,
Above the great walled girth of Joyous Gard
Spread forth its wide sad strength of shadow and gloom
Wherein those twain were compassed round with doom:
Hell from beneath called on them, and she heard
Reverberate judgment in the wild wind's word
Cry, till the sole sound of their names that rang
Clove all the sea-mist with a clarion's clang,
And clouds to clouds and flames to clustering flame.

Beat back the dark noise of the direful names.
Fear and strong exultation caught her breath,
And triumph like the bitterness of death,
And rapture like the rage of hate allayed
With ruin and ravin that its might hath made;
And her heart swelled and strained itself to hear
What may be heard of no man's hungering ear,
And as a soil that cleaves in twain for drought
Thirsted for judgment given of God's own mouth
Against them, till the strength of dark desire
Was in her as a flame of hell's own fire.
Nor seemed the wrath which held her spirit in stress
Aught else or worse than passionate holiness,
Nor the ardent hate which called on judgment's rod
More hateful than the righteousness of God.

"How long, till thou do justice, and my wrong
Stand expiate? O long-suffering judge, how long?
Shalt thou not put him in mine hand one day
Whom I so loved, to spare not but to slay?
Shalt thou not cast her down for me to tread,
Me, on the pale pride of her humbled head?
Do I not well, being angry? doth not hell
Require them? yea, thou knowest that I do well.
Is not thy seal there set of bloodred light
For witness on the brows of day and night?
Who shall unseal it? what shall melt away
Thy signet from the doors of night and day?
No man, nor strength of any spirit above,
Nor prayer, nor ardours of adulterous love.
Thou art God, the strong lord over body and soul:
Hast thou not in the terrors of thy scroll
All names of all men written as with fire?
Thine only breath bids time and space respire:
And are not all things evil in them done
More clear in thine eyes than in ours the sun?
Hast thou not sight stretched wide enough to see
These that offend it, these at once and me?
Is thine arm shortened or thine hand struck down
As palsied? have thy brows not strength to frown?
Are thine eyes blind with film of withering age?
Burns not thine heart with righteousness of rage
Yet, and the royal rancour toward thy foes
Retributive of ruin? Time should close,
Thou said'st, and earth fade as a leaf grows grey,
Was this then not thy word, thou God most high,
That sin shall surely bring forth death and die,
Seeing how these twain live and have joy of life,

His harlot and the man that made me wife?
For is it I, perchance, I that have sinned?
Me, peradventure, should thy wasting wind
Smite, and thy sun blast, and thy storms devour
Me with keen fangs of lightning? should thy power
Put forth on me the weight of its awakening hour?
Shall I that bear this burden bear that weight
Of judgment? is my sin against thee great,
If all my heart against them burn with all its hate?
Thine, and not mine, should hate be? nay, but me
They have spoiled and scoffed at, who can touch not thee.
Me, me, the fullness of their joy drains dry,
Their fruitfulness makes barren: thou, not I,
Lord, is it, whom their wrongdoing clothes with shame
That all who speak shoot tongues out at thy name
As all who hear mock mine? Make me thy sword
At least, if even thou too be wronged, O Lord,
At all of these that wrong me: make mine hand
As lightning, or my tongue a fiery brand,
To burn or smite them with thy wrath: behold,
I have nought on earth save thee for hope or hold,
Fair me not thou: I have nought but this to crave,
Make me thy mean to give them to the grave,
Thy sign that all men seeing may speak thee just,
Thy word which turns the strengths of sin to dust,
Thy blast which burns up towers and thrones with fire.
Lord, is this gift, this grace that I require,
So great a gift, Lord, for thy grace to give
And bid me bear thy part retributive?
That I whom scorn makes mouths at, I might be
Thy witness if loud sin may mock at thee?
For lo, my life is as a barren ear
Plucked from the sheaf: dark days drive past me here
Downtrodden, while joy's reapers pile their sheaves,
A thing more vile than autumn's weariest leaves,
For these the sun filled once with sap of life.
O thou my lord that hadst me to thy wife,
Dost thou not fear at all, remembering me,
The love that bowed my whole soul down to thee?
Is this so wholly nought for man to dread,
Man, whose life walks between the quick and dead,
Naked, and warred about with wind and sea,
That one should love and hate as I do thee?
That one should live in all the world his foe
So mortal as the hate that loves him so?
Nought, is it nought, O husband, O my knight,
O strong man and indomitable in fight,
That one more weak than foam-bells on the sea

Should have in heart such thoughts as I of thee?
Thou art bound about with stately strengths for bands:
What strength shall keep thee from my strengthless hands?
Thou art girt about with goodly guards and great:
What fosse may fence thee round as deep as hate?
Thou art wise: will wisdom teach thee fear of me?
Thou art great of heart: shall this deliver thee?
What wall so massive, or what tower so high
Shall be thy surety that thou shouldst not die,
If that which comes against thee be but I?
Who shall rise up of power to take thy part,
What skill find strength to save, what strength find art,
If that which wars against thee be my heart?
Not iron, nor the might of force afield,
Nor edge of sword, nor sheltering weight of shield,
Nor all the love and laud thou hast of man,
Nor, though his noiseless hours with wool be shod,
Shall God's love keep thee from the wrath of God.
O son of sorrows, hast thou said at heart,
Haply, God loves thee, God shall take thy part,
Who hath all these years endured thee, since thy birth
From sorrow's womb bade sin be born on earth?
So long he hath cast his buckler over thee,
Shall he not surely guard thee even from me?
Yea, but if yet he give thee while I live
Into mine hands as he shall surely give,
Ere death at last bring darkness on thy face,
Call then on him, call not on me for grace,
Cast not away one prayer, one suppliant breath,
On me that was commune all this while with death.
For I that was not and that was thy wife
Desire not but one hour of all thy life
Wherein to triumph till that hour be past;
But this mine hour I look for is thy last."

So mused she till the fire in sea and sky
Sank, and the northwest wind spake harsh on high,
And like the sea's heart waxed her heart that heard,
Strong, dark, and bitter, till the keen wind's word
Seemed of her own soul spoken, and the breath
All round her not of darkness, but of death.

VIII

THE LAST PILGRIMAGE

Enough of ease, O Love, enough of light,
Enough of rest before the shadow of night.
Strong Love, whom death finds feebler; kingly Love,
Whom time discrowns in season, seeing thy dove
Spell-stricken by the serpent; for thy sake
These that saw light see night's dawn only break,
Night's cup filled up with slumber, whence men think
The draught more dread than thine was dire to drink.
O Love, thy day sets darkling: hope and fear
Fall from thee standing stern as death stands here.

For what have these to do with fear or hope
On whom the gates of outer darkness ope,
One whom the door of life's desire is barred?
Past like a cloud, their days in Joyous Gard
Gleam like a cloud the westering sun stains red
Till all the blood of day's blithe heart be bled
And all night's heart requickened; in their eyes
So flame and fade those far memorial skies,
So shines the moorland, so revives the sea,
Wheron they gazing mused of things to be
And wist not more of them than waters know
What wind with next day's change of tide shall blow.
Dark roll the deepening days whose waves divide
Unseasonably, with storm-struck change of tide,
Tristram from Iseult: nor may sorrow say
If better wind shall blow than yesterday
With next day risen or any day to come.
For ere the songs of summer's death fell dumb,
And autumn bade the imperial moorlands change
Their purples, and the bracken's bloom grow strange
As hope's green blossom touched with time's harsh rust,
Was all their joy of life shaken to dust,
And all its fire made ashes: by the strand
Where late they strayed and communed hand from hand
For the last time fell separate, eyes of eyes
Took for the last time leave, and saw the skies
Dark with their deep division. The last time —
The last that ever love's rekindling rhyme
Should keep for them life's days and nights in tune
With refluence of the morning and the moon
Alternative in music, and make one
The secrets of the stardawn and the sun
For these twain souls ere darkness held them fast;
The last before the labour marked for last
And toil of utmost knighthood, till the wage
Of rest might crown his crowning pilgrimage
Whereon forth faring must he take farewell,

With spear for staff and sword for scallop-shell
And scrip wherein close memory hoarded yet
Things holier held than death might well forget;
The last time ere the travel were begun
Whose goal is unbeholden of the sun,
The last wherewith love's eyes might yet be lit,
Came, and they could but dream they knew not it.

For Tristram parting from her wist at heart
How well she wist they might not choose but part,
And he pass forth a pilgrim, when there came
A sound of summons in the high king's name
For succour toward his vassal Triamour,
King in wild Wales, now spoiled of all his power,
As Tristram's father ere his fair son's birth,
By one the strongest of the sons of earth,
Urgan, an iron bulk of giant mould:
And Iseult in Tintagel as of old
Sat crowned with state and sorrow: for her lord
At Arthur's hand required her back restored,
And willingly compelled against her will
She yielded, saying within her own soul still
Some season yet of soft or stormier breath
Should haply give her life again or death:
For now nor quick nor dead nor bright nor dark
Were all her nights and days wherein King Mark
Held haggard watch upon her, and his eyes
Were cloudier than the gradual wintering skies
That closed about the wan wild land and sea.
And bitter toward him waxed her heart: but he
Was rent in twain betwixt harsh love and hate
With pain and passion half compassionate
That yearned and laboured to be quit of shame,
And could not: and his life grew smouldering flame,
And hers a cloud full-charged with storm and shower,
Though touched with trembling gleams of fire's bright flower
That flashed and faded on its fitful verge,
As hope would strive with darkness and emerge
And sink, a swimmer strangled by the swallowing surge.

But Tristram by dense hills and deepening vales
Rode through the wild glad wastes of glorious Wales,
High-hearted with desire of happy fight
And strong in soul with merrier sense of might
Than since the fair first years that hailed him knight:
For all his will was toward the war, so long
Had love repressed and wrought his glory wrong,
So far the triumph and so fair the praise

Seemed now that kindled all his April days.
And here in bright blown autumn, while his life
Was summer's yet for strength toward love or strife,
Blithe waxed his hope toward battle, and high desire
To pluck once more as out of circling fire
Fame, the broad flower whose breath makes death more sweet
Than roses crushed by love's receding feet.
But all the lovely land wherein he went
The blast of ruin and ravenous war had rent;
And black with fire the fields where homesteads were,
And foul with festering dead the high soft air,
And loud with wail of women many a stream
Whose own live song was like love's deepening dream,
Spake all against the spoiler: wherefore still
Wrath waxed with pity, quickening all his will,
In Tristram's heart for every league he rode
Through the aching land so broad a curse bestrode
With so supreme a shadow: till one dawn
Above the green bloom of a gleaming lawn,
High on the strait steep windy bridge that spanned
A glen's deep mouth, he saw that shadow stand
Visible, sword on thigh and mace in hand
Vast as the mid bulk of a roof-tree's beam.
So, sheer above the wild wolf-haunted stream,
Dire as the face disfeatured of a dream
Rose Urgan: and his eyes were night and flame;
But like the fiery dawn were his that came
Against him, lit with more sublime desire
Than lifts toward heaven the leaping heart of fire:
And strong in vantage of his perilous place
The huge high presence, red as earth's first race,
Reared like a reed the might up of his mace,
And smote: but lightly Tristram swerved, and drove
Right in on him, whose void stroke only clove
Air, and fell wide, thundering athwart: and he
Sent forth a stormier cry than wind or sea
When midnight takes the tempest for her lord
And all the glen's throat seemed as hell's that roared;
But high like heaven's light over hell shone Tristram's sword,
Falling, and bright as storm shows God's bare brand
Flashed as it shore sheer off the huge right hand
Whose strength was as the shadow of death on all that land.
And like the trunk of some grim tree sawn through
Reeled Urgan, as his left hand grasped and drew
A steel by sorcerers tempered: and anew
Raged the red wind of fluctuant fight, till all
The cliffs were thrilled as by the clangorous call
Of storm's blown trumpets from the core of night,

Charging: and even as with the storm-wind's might
On Tristram's helm that sword crashed: and the knight
Fell, and his arms clashed, and a wide cry brake
From those far off that heard it, for his sake
Soul-stricken: and that bulk of monstrous birth
Sent forth again a cry more dire for mirth:
But ere the sunbright arms were soiled of earth
They flashed again, re-risen: and swift and loud
Rang the strokes out as from a circling cloud,
So dense the dust wrought over them its drifted shroud.
Strong strokes, within the mist their battle made,
Each hailed on other through the shifting shade
That clung about them hurtling as the swift fight swayed:
And each between the jointed corslet saw
Break forth his foe's bright blood at each grim flaw
Steel made in hammered iron: till again
The fiend put forth his might more strong for pain
And cleft the great knight's glittering shield in twain,
Laughing for very wrath and thirst to kill,
A beast's broad laugh of blind and wolfish will,
And smote again ere Tristram's lips drew breath
Panting, and swept as by the sense of death,
That surely should have touched and sealed them fast
Save that the sheer stroke shrilled aside, and passed
Frustrate: but answering Tristram smote anew,
And thrust the brute beast as with lightning through
Clean with one cleaving stroke of perfect might:
And violently the vast bulk leapt upright,
And plunged over the bridge, and fell: and all
The cliffs reverberate from his monstrous fall
Rang: and the land by Tristram's grace was free.
So with high laud and honour thence went he,
And southward set his sail again, and passed
The lone land's ending, first beheld and last
Of eyes that look on England from the sea:
And his heart mourned within him, knowing how she
Whose heart with his was fateful made fast
Sat now fast bound, as though some charm were cast
About her, such a brief space eastward thence,
And yet might soul not break the bonds of sense
And bring her to him in very life and breath
More than had this been even the sea of death
That washed between them, and its wide sweet light
The dim strait's darkness of the narrowing night
That shuts about men dying whose souls put forth
To pierce its passage through: but south and north
Alike for him were other than they were:
For all the northward coast shone smooth and fair,

And off its iron cliffs the keen-edged air
Blew summer, kindling from her mute bright mouth;
But winter breathed out of the murmuring south
Where, pale with wrathful watch on passing ships,
The lone wife lay in wait with wan dumb lips.
Yet, sailing where the shoreward ripple curled
Of the most wild sweet waves in all the world
His soul took comfort even for joy to see
The strong deep joy of living sun and sea,
The large deep love of living sea and land,
As past the lonely lion-guarded strand
Where the huge warder lifts his couchant sides,
Asleep, above the sleepless lapse of tides,
The light sail swept, and past the unsounded caves
Unsearchable, wherein the pulse of waves
Throbs through perpetual darkness to and fro,
And the blind night swims heavily below
While heavily the strong noon broods above,
Even to the very bay whence very Love,
Strong daughter of the giant gods who wrought
Sun, earth, and sea out of their procreant thought,
Most meetly might have risen, and most divine
Beheld and heard things round her sound and shine
From floors of foam and gold to walls of serpentine.
For splendid as the limbs of that supreme
Incarnate beauty through men's visions gleam,
Whereof all fairest things are even but shadow or dream,
And lovely like as Love's own heavenliest face,
Gleams there and glows the presence and the grace
Even of the mother of all, in perfect pride of place.
For otherwhere beneath our world-wide sky
There may not be beheld of men that die
Aught else like this that dies not, nor may stress
Of ages that bow down men's works make less
The exultant awe that clothes with power its loveliness.
For who sets eye thereon soever knows
How since these rocks and waves first rolled and rose
The marvel of their many-coloured might
Hath borne this record sensible to sight,
The witness and the symbol of their own delight,
The gospel graven of life's most heavenly law,
Joy, brooding on its own still soul with awe,
A sense of godlike rest in godlike strife,
The sovereign conscience of the spirit of life.
Nor otherwhere on strand or mountain tower
Hath such fair beauty shining forth in flower
Put on the imperial robe of such imperious power.
For all the radiant rocks from depth to height

Burn with vast bloom of glories blossom-bright
As though the sun's own hand had thrilled them through with light
And stained them through with splendour: yet from thence
Such awe strikes rapture through the spirit of sense
From all the inaccessible sea-wall's girth,
That exultation, bright at heart as mirth,
Bows deeper down before the beauty of earth
Than fear may bow down ever: nor shall one
Who meets at Alpine dawn the mounting sun
On heights too high for many a wing to climb
Be touched with sense of aught seen more sublime
Than here smiles high and sweet in face of heaven and time.
For here the flower of fire, the soft hoar bloom
Of springtide olive-woods, the warm green gloom
Of clouded seas that swell and sound with dawn of doom,
The keen thwart lightning and the wan grey light
Of stormy sunrise crossed and vexed with night,
Flash, loom, and laugh with divers hues in one
From all the curved cliff's face, till day be done,
Against the sea's face and the gazing sun.
And whensoever a strong wave, high in hope,
Sweeps up some smooth slant breadth of stone aslope,
That glowed with duskier fire of hues less bright,
Swift as it sweeps back springs to sudden sight
The splendour of the moist rock's fervent light,
Fresh as from dew of birth when time was born
Our of the world-conceiving womb of morn.
All its quenched flames and darkling hues divine
Leap into lustrous life and laugh and shine
And darken into swift and dim decline
For one brief breath's space till the next wave run
And leave it to be kissed and kindled of the sun.
And all these things, bright as they shone before
Man first set foot on earth or sail from shore,
Rose not less radiant than the sun sees now
When the autumn sea was cloven of Tristram's prow,
And strong in sorrow and hope and woful will
That hope might move not nor might sorrow kill
He held his way back toward the wild sad shore
Whence he should come to look on these no more,
Nor ever, save with sunless eyes shut fast,
Sail home to sleep in home-born earth at last.

And all these things fled fleet as light or breath
Past, and his heart waxed cold and dull as death,
Or swelled but as the tides of sorrow swell,
To sing with sullen sense of slow farewell.
So surely seemed the silence even to sigh

Assurance of inveterate prophesy,
"Thou shalt not come again home hither ere thou die."
And the wind mourned and triumphed, and the sea
Wailed and took heart and trembled; nor might he
Hear more of comfort in their speech, or see
More certitude in all the waste world's range
Than the only certitude of death and change.
And as the sense and semblance fluctuated
Of all things heard and seen alive or dead
That smote far off upon his ears or eyes
Or memory mixed with forecasts fain to rise
And fancies faint as ghostliest prophecies,
So seemed his own soul, changefully forlorn,
To shrink and triumph and mount up and mourn;
Yet all its fitful waters, clothed with night,
Lost heart not wholly, lacked not wholly light,
Seeing over life and death one star in sight
Where evening's gates as fair as morning's ope,
Whose name was memory, but whose flame was hope.
For all the tides of thought that rose and sank
Felt its fair strength wherefrom strong sorrow shrank
A mightier trust than time could change or cloy,
More strong than sorrow, more secure than joy.
So came he, nor content nor all unblest,
Back to the grey old land of Merlin's rest.

But ere six paces forth on shore he trod
Before him stood a knight with feet unshod,
And kneeling called upon him, as on God
Might sick men call for pity, praying aloud
With hands held up and head made bare and bowed;
"Tristram, for God's love and thine own dear fame,
I Tristram that am one with thee in name
And one in heart with all that praise thee—I,
Most woful man of all that may not die
For heartbreak and the heavier scourge of shame,
By all thy glory done our woful name
Beseech thee, called of all men gentlest knight,
Be now not slow to do my sorrows right.
I charge thee for thy fame's sake through this land,
I pray thee by thine own wife's fair white hand,
Have pity of me whose love is borne away
By one that makes of poor men's lives his prey,
A felon masked with knighthood: at his side
Seven brethren hath he night or day to ride
With seven knights more than wait on all his will:
And here at hand, ere yet one day fulfill
Its flight through light and darkness, shall they fare

Forth, and my bride among them, whom they bear
Through these wild lands his prisoner; and if now
I lose her, and my prayer be vain, and thou
Less fain to serve love's servants than of yore,
Then surely shall I see her face no more.
But if thou wilt, for love's sake of the bride
Who lay most loved of women at thy side,
Strike with me, straight then hence behoves us ride
And rest between the moorside and the sea
Where we may smite them passing: but for me,
Poor stranger, me not worthy scarce to touch
Thy kind strong hand, how shouldst thou do so much?
For now lone left this long time waits thy wife
And lacks her lord and light of wedded life
Whilst thou far off art famous: yet thy fame,
If thou take pity on me that bear thy name
Unworthily, but by that name implore
Thy grace, how shall not even thy fame grow more?
But be thy will as God's among us done,
Who art far in fame above us as the sun:
Yet only of him have all men help and grace."

And all the lordly light of Tristram's face
Was softened as the sun's in kindly spring.
"Nay, then may God send me as evil a thing
When I give ear not to such prayers," he said,
"And make my place among the nameless dead
When I put back one hour the time to smite
And do the unrighteous griefs of good men right.
Behold, I will not enter in nor rest
Here in mine own halls till this piteous quest
Find end ere noon to-morrow: but do thou,
Whose sister's face I may not look on now,
Go, Ganhardine, with tiding of the vow
That bids me turn aside for one day's strife
Or live dishonoured all my days of life,
And greet for me in brother's wise my wife,
And crave her pardon that for knighthood's sake
And womanhood's, whose bands may no man break
And keep the bands of bounden honour fast,
I seek not her till two nights yet be past
And this my quest accomplished, so God please
By me to give this young man's anguish ease
And on his wrongdoer's head his wrong requite."

And Tristram with that woful thankful knight
Rode by the seaside moorland wastes away
Between the quickening night and darkening day

Ere half the gathering stars had heart to shine.
And lightly toward his sister Ganhardine
Sped, where she sat and gazed alone afar
Above the grey sea for the sunset star,
And lightly kissed her hand and lightly spake
His tiding of that quest for knighthood's sake.
And the white-handed Iseult, bowing her head,
Gleamed on him with a glance athwart, and said,
"As God's on earth and far above the sun,
So toward his handmaid be my lord's will done."
And doubts too dim to question or divine
Touched as with shade the spirit of Ganhardine,
Hearing; and scarce for half a doubtful breath
His bright light heart held half a thought of death
And knew not whence this darkling thought might be,
But surely not his sister's work: for she
Was ever sweet and good as summer air,
And soft as dew when all the night is fair,
And gracious as the golden maiden moon
When darkness craves her blessing: so full soon
His mind was light again as leaping waves,
Nor dreamed that hers was like a field of graves
Where no man's foot dares swerve to left or right,
Nor ear dares hearken, nor dares eye take sight
Of aught that moves and murmurs there at night.

But by the sea-banks where at morn their foes
Might find them, lay those knightly name-fellows,
One sick with grief of heart and sleepless, one
With heart of hope triumphant as the sun
Dreaming asleep of love and fame and fight:
But sleep at last wrapped warm the wan young knight;
And Tristram with the first pale windy light
Woke ere the sun spake summons, and his ear
Caught the sea's call that fired his heart to hear,
A noise of waking waters: for till dawn
The sea was silent as a mountain lawn
When the wind speaks not, and the pines are dumb
And summer takes her fill ere autumn come
Of life more soft than slumber: but ere day
Rose, and the first beam smote the bounding bay,
Up sprang the strength of the dark East, and took
With its wide wings the waters as they shook,
And hurled them huddling on aheap, and cast
The full sea shoreward with a great glad blast,
Blown from the heart of morning: and with joy
Full-souled and perfect passion, as a boy
That leaps up light to wrestle with the sea

For pure heart's gladness and large ecstasy,
Up sprang the might of Tristram: and his soul
Yearned for delight within him, and waxed whole
As a young child's with rapture of the hour
That brought his spirit and all the world to flower,
And all the bright blood in his veins beat time
To the wind's clarion and the water's chime
That called him and he followed it and stood
On the sand's verge before the great grey flood
Where the white hurtling heads of waves that met
Rose unsaluted of the sunrise yet.
And from his heart's root outward shot the sweet
Strong joy that thrilled him to the hands and feet,
Filling his limbs with pleasure and glad might,
And his soul drank the immeasurable delight
That earth drinks in with morning, and the free
Limitless love that lifts the stirring sea
When on her bare bright bosom as a bride
She takes the young sun, perfect in his pride,
Home to his place with passion: and the heart
Trembled for joy within the man whose part
Was here not least in living; and his mind
Was rapt abroad beyond man's meaner kind
And pierced with love of all things and with mirth
Moved to make one with heaven and heavenlike earth
And with the light live water. So awhile
He watched the dim sea with a deepening smile,
And felt the sound and savour and swift flight
Of waves that fled beneath the fading night
And died before the darkness, like a song
With harps between and trumpets blown along
Through the loud air of some triumphant day,
Sink through his spirit and purge all sense away
Save of the glorious gladness of his hour
And all the world about the break in flower
Before the sovereign laughter of the sun;
And he, ere night's wide work lay all undone,
As earth from her bright body casts off night,
Cast off his raiment for a rapturous fight
And stood between the sea's edge and the sea
Naked, and godlike of his mould as he
Whose swift foot's sound shook all the towers of Troy;
So clothed with might, so girt upon with joy
As, ere the knife had shorn to feed the fire
His glorious hair before the unkindled pyre
Whereon the half of his great heart was laid,
Stood, in the light of his live limbs arrayed,
Child of heroic earth and heavenly sea,

The flower of all men: scarce less bright than he,
If any of all men latter-born might stand,
Stood Tristram, silent, on the glimmering strand.
Not long: but with a cry of love that rang
As from a trumpet golden-mouthed he sprang,
As toward a mother's where his head might rest
That none may gird nor measure: and his heart
Sent forth a shout that bade his lips not part,
But triumphed in him silent: no man's voice,
No song, no sound of clarions that rejoice,
Can set that glory forth which fills with fire
The body and soul that have their whole desire
Silent, and freer than birds or dreams are free
Take all their will of all the encountering sea.
And toward the foam he bent and forward smote,
Laughing, and launched his body like a boat
Full to the sea-breach, and against the tide
Struck strongly forth with amorous arms make wide
To take the bright breast of the wave to his
And on his lips the sharp sweet minute's kiss
Given of the wave's lip for a breath's space curled
And pure as at the daydawn of the world.
And round him all the bright rough shuddering sea
Kindled, as though the world were even as he,
Heart-stung with exultations of desire:
And all the life that moved him seemed to aspire,
As all the sea's life toward the sun: and still
Delight within him waxed with quickening will
More smooth and strong and perfect as a flame
That springs and spreads, till each glad limb became
A note of rapture in the tune of life,
Live music mild and keen as sleep and strife:
Till the sweet change that bids the sense grow sure
Of deeper depth and purity more pure
Wrapped him and lapped him round with clearer cold,
And all the rippling green grew royal gold
Between him and the far sun's rising rim.
And like the sun his heart rejoiced in him,
And brightened with a broadening flame of mirth:
But the life kindled of a fiery birth
And passion of a new-begotten son
Between the live sea and the living sun.
And mightier grew the joy to meet full-faced
Each wave, and mount with upward plunge, and taste
The rapture of its rolling strength, and cross
Its flickering crown of snows that flash and toss
Like plumes in battle's blithest charge, and thence
To match the next with yet more strenuous sense;

Till on his eyes the light beat hard and bade
His face turn west and shoreward through the glad
Swift revel of the waters golden-clad,
And back with light reluctant heart he bore
Across the broad-backed rollers in to shore;
Strong-spirited for the chance and cheer of fight,
And donned his arms again, and felt the might
In all his limbs rejoice for strength, and praised
God for such life as that wheron he gazed,
And wist not surely its joy was even as fleet
As that which laughed and lapsed against his feet,
The bright thin grey foam-blossom, glad and hoar,
That flings its flower along the flowerless shore
On sand or shingle, and still with sweet strange snows,
As where one great white storm-dishevelled rose
May rain her wild leaves on a windy land,
Strews for long leagues the sounding slope of strand
And flower on flower falls flashing, and anew
A fresh light leaps up whence the last flash flew,
And casts its brief glad gleam of life away
To fade not flowerwise but as drops the day
Storm-smitten, when at once the dark devours
Heaven and the sea and earth with all their flowers;
No star in heaven, on earth no rose to see,
But the white blown brief blossoms of the sea,
That make her green gloom starrier than the sky,
Dance yet before the tempest's tune, and die.
And all these things he glanced upon, and knew
How fair they shone, from earth's least flake of dew
To stretch of seas and imminence of skies,
Unwittingly, with unpresageful eyes,
For the last time. The world's half heavenly face,
The music of the silence of the place,
The confluence and the refluence of the sea,
The wind's note ringing over wold and lea,
Smote once more through him keen as fire that smote,
Rang once more through him one reverberate note,
That faded as he turned again and went,
Fulfilled by strenuous joy with strong content,
To take his last delight of labour done
That yet should be beholden of the sun
Or ever give man comfort of his hand.

Beside a wood's edge in the broken land
An hour at wait the twain together stood,
Till swift between the moorside and the wood
Flashed the spears forward of the coming train;
And seeing beside the strong chief spoiler's rein

His wan love riding prisoner in the crew,
Forth with a cry the young man leapt, and flew
Right on that felon sudden as a flame;
And hard at hand the mightier Tristram came,
Bright as the sun and terrible as fire:
And there had sword and spear their soul's desire,
And blood that quenched the spear's thirst as it poured
Slaked royally the hunger of the sword,
Till the fierce heat of steel could scarce fulfil
Its greed and ravin of insatiate will.
For three the fiery spear of Tristram drove
Down ere a point of theirs his harness clove
Or its own sheer mid shaft splintered in twain
And his heart bounded in him , and was fain
As fire or wind that takes its fill by night
Of tempest and of triumph: so the knight
Rejoiced and ranged among them, great of hand,
Till seven lay slain upon the heathery sand
Or in the dense breadth of the woodside fern.
Nor did his heart not mightier in him burn
Seeing at his hand that young knight fallen, and high
The red sword reared again that bade him die.
But on the slayer exulting like the flame
Whose foot foreshines the thunder Tristram came
Raging, for piteous wrath had made him fire;
And as a lion's look his face was dire
That flashed against his foeman ere the sword
Lightened and wrought the heart's will of its lord
And clove through casque and crown the wrongdoer's head.
And right and left about their dark chief dead
Hurtled and hurled those felons to and fro,
Till as a storm-wind scatters leaves and snow
His right hand ravening scattered them; but one
That fled with sidelong glance athwart the sun
Shot, and the shaft flew sure, and smote aright,
Full in the wound's print of his great first fight
When at his young strength's peril he made free
Cornwall, and slew beside its bordering seas
The fair land's foe, who yielding up his breath
Yet left him wounded night to dark slow death.
And hardly with long toil thence he won home
Between the grey moor and the glimmering foam,
And halting fared through his own gate, and fell,
Thirsting: for as the sleepless fire of hell
The fire within him of his wound again
Burned, and his face was dark as death for pain,
And blind the blithe light of his eyes: but they
Within that watched wist not of the fray

Came forth and cried aloud on him for woe.
And scarce aloud his thanks fell faint and slow
As men reared up the strong man fallen and bore
Down the deep hall that looked along the shore,
And laid him soft abed, and sought in vain
If herb or hand of leech might heal his pain.
And the white-handed Iseult hearkening heard
All, and drew night, and spake no wifely word,
But gazed upon his doubtfully, with eyes
Clouded; and he in kindly knightly wise
Spake with scant breath, and smiling: "Surely this
Is penance for discourteous lips to kiss
And feel the brand burn through them, here to lie
And lack the strength here to do more than sigh
And hope not hence for pardon." Then she bowed
Her head, still silent as a stooping cloud,
And laid her lips against his face; and he
Felt sink a shadow across him as the sea
Might feel a cloud stoop toward it: and his heart
Darkened as one that wastes by sorcerous art
And knows not whence it withers: and he turned
Back from her emerald eyes his own, and yearned
All night for eyes all golden: and the dark
Hung sleepless round him till the loud first lark
Rang record forth once more of darkness done,
And all things born took comfort from the sun.

IX

THE SAILING OF THE SWAN

Fate, that was born ere spirit and flesh were made,
The fire that fills man's life with light and shade;
The power beyond all godhead which puts on
All forms of multitudinous unison,
A raiment of eternal change inwrought
With shapes and hues more subtly spun than thought,
Where all things old bear fruit of all things new
And one deep chord throbs all the music through,
The chord of change unchanging, shadow and light
Inseparable as reverberate day from night;
Fate, that of all things save the soul of man
Is lord and God since body and soul began;
Fate, that breathes power upon the lips of time;
That smites and soothes with heavy and healing hand
All joys and sorrows born in life's dim land,

Till joy be found a shadow and sorrow a breath
And life no discord in the tune with death,
But all things fain alike to die and live
In pulse and lapse of tides alternative,
Through silence and through sound of peace and strife
Till birth and death be one in sight of life;
Fate, heard and seen of no man's eyes or ears,
To no man shown through light of smiles or tears,
And moved of no man's prayer to fold its wings;
Fate, that is night and light on worldly things;
Fate, that is fire to burn and sea to drown,
Strength to build up and thunder to cast down;
Fate, shield and screen for each man's lifelong head,
And sword at last or dart that strikes it dead,
Fate, higher than heaven and deeper than the grave,
That saves and spares not, spares and doth not save;
Fate, that in gods'wise is not bought and sold
For prayer or price of penitence or gold;
Whose law shall live when life bids earth farewell,
Whose justice hath for shadows heaven and hell
Whose judgment into no god's hand is given,
Nor is its doom not more than hell or heaven:
Fate, that is pure of love and clean of hate,
Being equal-eyed as nought may be but fate;
Through many and weary days of foiled desire
Leads life to rest where tears no more take fire;
Through many and weary dreams of quenched delight
Leads life through death past sense of day and night.

Nor shall they feel or fear, whose date is done,
Aught that made once more dark the living sun
And bitterer in their breathing lips the breath
Than the dark dawn and bitter dust of death.
For all the light, with fragrance as of flowers,
That clothes the lithe live limbs of separate hours,
More sweet to savour and more clear to sight
Dawns on the soul death's undivided night.
No vigils has that perfect night to keep,
No fever-fits of vision shake that sleep.
Nor if they wake, and any place there be
Wherein the soul may feel her wings beat free
Through air too clear and still for sound or strife
If life were haply death, and death be life;
If love with yet some lovelier laugh revive,
And song relume the light it bore alive,
And friendship, found of all earth's gifts most good,
If aught indeed at all of all this be,
Though none might say nor any man might see,

Might he that sees the shade thereof not say
This dream were trustier than the truth of day.
Nor haply may not hope, with heart more clear,
Burn deathward, and the doubtful soul take cheer,
Seeing through the channelled darkness yearn a star
Whose eyebeams are not as the morning's are,
Transient, and subjugate of lordlier light,
But all unconquerable by noon or night,
Being kindled only of life's own inmost fire,
Truth, stablished and made sure by strong desire
Fountain of all things living, source and seed,
Force that perforce transfigures dream to deed
God that begets on time, the body of death,
Eternity: nor may man's darkening breath,
Albeit it stain, disfigure or destroy
The glass wherein the soul sees life and joy
Only, with strength renewed and spirit of youth,
And brighter than the sun's the body of Truth
Eternal, unimaginable of man,
Whose very face not Thought's own eyes may scan,
But see far off his radiant feet at least,
Trampling the head of Fear, the false high priest,
Whose broken chalice foams with blood no more,
And prostrate on that high priest's chancel floor,
Bruised, overthrown, blind, maimed, with bloodless rod,
The miscreation of his miscreant God.
That sovereign shadow cast of souls that dwell
In darkness and the prison-house of hell
Whose walls are built of deadly dread, and bound
The gates thereof with dreams as iron round,
And all the bars therin and stanchions wrought
Of shadow forged like steel and tempered thought
And words like swords and thunder-clouded creeds
And faiths more dire than sin's most direful deeds:
That shade accursed and worshipped, which hath made
The soul of man that brought it forth a shade
Black as the womb of darkness, void and vain,
A throne for fear, a pasturage for pain,
Impotent, abject, clothed upon with lies,
A foul blind fume of words and prayers that rise,
Aghast and harsh, abhorrent and abhorred,
Fierce as its God, blood-saturate as its Lord;
With loves and mercies on its lips that hiss
Comfort, and kill compassion with a kiss,
And strike the world black with their blasting breath;
That ghost whose core of life is very death
And all its light of heaven a shadow of hell,
Fades, falls, wanes, withers by none other spell

But theirs whose eyes and ears have seen and heard
Not the face naked, not the perfect word,
But the bright sound and feature felt from far
Of life which feeds the spirit and the star,
Thrills the live light of all the suns that roll,
And stirs the still sealed springs of every soul.

Three dim days through, three slumberless nights long,
Perplexed at dawn, oppressed at evensong,
The strong man's soul now sealed indeed with pain
And all its springs half dried with drought, had lain
Prisoner within the fleshly dungeon-dress
Sore chafed and wasted with its weariness.
And fain it would have found the star, and fain
Made this funereal prison-house of pain
A watch-tower whence its eyes might sweep, and see
If any place for any hope might be
Beyond the hells and heavens of sleep and strife,
Or any light at all of any life
Beyond the dense false darkness woven above,
And could not, lacking grace to look on love,
And in the third night's dying hour he spake,
Seeing scarce the seals that bound the dayspring break
And scarce the daystar burn above the sea:
"O Ganhardine, my brother true to me,
I charge thee by those nights and days we knew
No great while since in England, by the dew
That bathed those nights with blessing, and the fire
That thrilled those days as music thrills a lyre,
Do now for me perchance the last good deed
That ever love may crave or life may need
Ere love lay life in ashes: take to thee
My ship that shows aloft against the sea
Carved on her stem the semblance of a swan,
And ere the waves at even again wax wan
Pass, if it may be, to my lady's land,
And give this ring into her secret hand,
And bid her think how hard on death I lie,
And fain would look upon her face and die.
But as a merchant's laden be the bark
With royal ware for fraughtage, that King Mark
May take for toll thereof some costly thing;
And when this gift finds grace before the king,
Choose forth a cup, and put therein my ring
Where sureliest only of one it may be seen,
And bid her handmaid bear it to the queen
For earnest of thine homage: then shall she
Fear, and take counsel privily with thee,

To know what errand there is thine from me
And what my need in secret of her sight.
But make thee two sails, one like sea-foam white
To spread for signal if thou bring her back,
And if she come not see the sail be black,
That I may know or ever thou take land
If these my lips may die upon her hand
Or hers may never more be mixed with mine."

And his heart quailed for grief in Ganhardine,
Hearing; and all his brother bade he swore
Surely to do, and straight fare forth from shore.
But the white-handed Iseult hearkening heard
All, and her heart waxed hot, and every world
Thereon seemed graven and printed in her thought
As lines with fire and molten iron wrought.
And hard within her heavy heart she cursed
Both, and her life was turned to fiery thirst,
And all her soul was hunger, and its breath
Of hope and life a blast of raging death.
For only in hope of evil was her life.
So bitter burned within the unchilded wife
A virgin lust for vengeance, and such hate
Wrought in her now the fervent work of fate.

Then with a south-west wind the Swan set forth
And over wintering waters bore to north,
And round the wild land's windy westward end
Up the blown channel bade her bright way bend
East on toward high Tintagel: where at dark
Landing, fair welcome found they of King Mark,
And Ganhardine with Brangwain as of old
Spake, and she took the cup of chiselled gold
Wherein lay secret Tristram's trothplight ring,
And bare it unbeholden of the king
Even to her lady's hand, which hardly took
A gift whereon a queen's eyes well might look,
With grace forlorn of weary gentleness.
But, seeing, her life leapt in her, keen to guess
The secret of the symbol: and her face
Flushed bright with blood whence all its grief-worn grace
Took fire and kindled to the quivering hair.
And in the dark soft hour of starriest air
Thrilled through with sense of midnight, when the world
Feels the wide wings of sleep about it furled,
Down stole the queen, deep-muffled to her war
Mute restless lips, and came where yet the Swan
Swung fast at anchor: whence by starlight she

Hoised snowbright sails, and took the glimmering sea.

But all the long night long more keen and sore
His wound's grief waxed in Tristram evermore,
And heavier always hung his heart asway
Between dim fear and clouded hope of day.
And still with face and heart at silent strife
Beside him watched the maiden called his wife,
Patient, and spake not save when scarce he spake,
Murmuring with sense distraught and spirit awake
Speech bitterer than the words thereof were sweet:
And hatred thrilled her to the hands and feet,
Listening: for alway back reiterate came
The passionate faint burden of her name.
Nor ever through the labouring lips astir
Came any word of any thought of her.
But the soul wandering struggled and clung hard
Only to dreams of joy in Joyous Gard
Or wildwood nights beside the Cornish strand,
Or Merlin's holier sleep here hard at hand
Wrapped round with deep soft spells in dim Broceliande.
And with such thirst as joy's drained wine-cup leaves
When fear to hope as hope to memory cleaves
His soul desired the dewy sense of leaves,
The soft green smell of thickets drenched with dawn.
The faint slot kindling on the fiery lawn
As day's first hour made keen the spirit again
That lured and spurred on quest his hound Hodain,
The breeze, the bloom, the splendour and the sound,
That stung like fire the hunter and the hound.
The pulse of wind, the passion of the sea,
The rapture of the woodland: then would he
Sigh, and as one that fain would all be dead
Heavily turn his heavy-laden head
Back, and close eyes for comfort, finding none.
And fain he would have died or seen the sun,
Being sick at heart of darkness: yet afresh
Began the long strong strife of spirit and flesh
And branching pangs of thought whose branches bear
The bloodred fruit whose core is black, despair.
And the wind slackened and again grew great,
Palpitant as men's pulses palpitate
Between the flowing and ebbing tides of fate
That wash their lifelong waifs of weal and woe
Through night and light and twilight to and fro
Now as a pulse of hope its heartbeat throbbed,
Now like one stricken shrank and sank and sobbed,
Then, yearning as with child of death, put forth

A wail that filled the night up south and north
With woful sound of waters: and he said,
"So might the wind wail if the world were dead
And its wings wandered over nought but sea.
I would I knew she would not come to me,
For surely she will come not: then should I,
Once knowing I shall not look upon her, die.
I knew not life could so long breathe such breath
As I do. Nay, what grief were this, if death,
The sole sure friend of whom the whole world saith
He lies not, nor hath ever this been said,
That death would heal not grief—if death were dead
And all ways closed whence grief might pass with life!"

Then softly spake his watching virgin wife
Out of her heart, deep down below her breath:
"Fear not but death shall come—and after death
Judgment." And he that heard not answered her
Saying—Ah, but one there was, if truth not err,
For true men's trustful tongues have said it—one
Whom these mine eyes knew living while the sun
Looked yet upon him, and mine own ears heard
The deep sweet sound once of his godlike word—
Who sleeps and dies not, but with soft live breath
Takes always all the deep delight of death,
Through love's gift of a woman: but for me
Love's hand is not the hand of Nimue,
Love's word no still smooth murmur of the dove,
No kiss of peace for me the kiss of love.
Nor, whatsoe'er thy life's love ever give,
Dear, shall it ever bid me sleep or live;
Nor from thy brows and lips and living breast
As from his Nimue's shall my soul take rest;
Not rest but unrest hath our long love given—
Unrest on earth that wins not rest in heaven.
What rest may we take ever? what have we
Had ever more of peace than has the sea?
Has not our life been as a wind that blows
Through lonelier lands than rear the wild white rose
That each year sees requickened, but for us
Time once and twice hath here or there done thus
And left the next year following empty and bare?
What rose hath our last year's rose left for heir,
What wine our last year's vintage? and to me
More were one fleet forbidden sense of thee,
One perfume of thy present grace, one thought
Made truth one hour, ere all mine hours be nought,
One very word, breath, look, sign, touch of hand,

Than all the green leaves in Broceliande
Full of sweet sound, full of sweet wind and sun;
O God, thou knowest I would no more but one,
I would no more but once more ere I die
Find thus much mercy. Nay, but then were I
Happier than he whom there thy grace hath found,
For thine it must be, this that wraps him round,
Thine only, albeit a fiend's force gave him birth,
Thine that has given him heritage on earth
Of slumber-sweet eternity to keep
Fast in soft hold of everliving sleep.
Happier were I, more sinful man, than he,
Whom one love-worthier then than Nimue
Should with a breath make blest among the dead."

And the wan wedded maiden answering said,
Soft as hate speaks within itself apart:
"Surely ye shall not, ye that rent mine heart,
Being one in sin, in punishment be twain."

And the great knight that heard not spake again
And sighed, but sweet thought of sweet things gone by
Kindled with fire of joy the very sight
And touched it through with rapture: "Ay, this were
How much more than the sun and sunbright air,
How much more than the springtide, how much more
Than sweet strong sea-wind quickening wave and shore
With one divine pulse of continuous breath,
If she might kiss me with the kiss of death,
And make the light of life by death's look dim!"

And the white wedded virgin answered him,
Inwardly, wan with hurt no herb makes whole:
"Yea, surely, ye whose sin hath slain my soul,
Surely your own souls shall have peace in death
And pass with benediction into their breath
And blessing given of mine their sin hath slain."

And Tristram with sore yearning spake again,
Saying: "Yea, might this thing once be, how should I,
With all my soul made one thanksgiving, die,
And pass before what judgment-seat may be,
And cry, 'Lord, now do all thou wilt with me,
Take all thy fill of justice, work thy will;
Though all thy heart of wrath have all its fill,
My heart of suffering shall endure, and say,
For thou that gavest me living yesterday
I bless thee though thou curse me.' Ay, and well

Might one cast down into the gulf of hell,
Remembering this, take heart and thank his fate—
Once, in the wild and whirling world above,
Bade mercy kiss his dying lips with love.
But if this come not, then he doth me wrong.
For what hath love done, all this long life long
That death should trample down his poor last prayer
Who prays not for forgiveness? Though love were
Sin dark as hate, have we not here that sinned
Suffered? has that been less than wintry wind
Wherewith our love lies blasted? O mine own,
O mine and no man's yet save mine alone,
Iseult! what ails thee that I lack so long
All of thee, all things thine for which I long?
For more than watersprings to shadeless sands,
More to me were the comfort of her hands
Touched once, and more than rays that set and rise
The glittering arrows of her glorious eyes,
More to my sense than fire to dead cold air
The wind and light and odour of her hair,
More to my soul than summer's to the south
The mute clear music of her amorous mouth,
The fullness of the fragrance of her breast
And to my heart's heart more than heaven's great rest
Iseult, Iseult, what grace hath life to give
More than we twain have had of life, and live?
Iseult, Iseult, what grace may death not keep
As sweet for us to win of death, and sleep?
Come therefore, let us twain pass hence and try
If it be better not to live but die,
With love for lamp to light us out of life."

And on that word his wedded maiden wife,
Pale as the moon in star-forsaken skies
Ere the sun fill them, rose with set strange eyes
And gazed on him that saw not: and her heart
Heaved as a man's death-smitten with a dart
That smites him sleeping, warm and full of life:
So toward her lord that was not looked his wife,
His wife that was not: and her heart within
Burnt bitter like an aftertaste of sin
To one whose memory drinks and loathes the lee
Of shame or sorrow deeper than the sea:
And no fear touched him of her eyes above
And ears that hoarded each poor word whence love
Made sweet the broken music of his breath.
"Iseult, my life that wast and art my death,
My life in life that hast been, and that art

Death in my death, sole wound that cleaves mine heart,
Mine heart that else, how spent soe'er, were whole,
Breath of my sprit and anguish of my soul,
How can this be that hence thou canst not hear,
Being but by space divided? One is here,
But one of twain I looked at once to see;
Shall death keep time and thou not keep with me?"

And the white married maiden laughed at heart,
Hearing, and scarce with lips at all apart
Spake, and as fire between them was her breath;
"Yea, now thou liest not: yea, for I am death."

By this might eyes that watched without behold
Deep in the gulfs of aching air acold
The roses of the dawning heaven that strew
The low soft sun's way ere his power shine through
And burn them up with fire: but far to west
Had sunk the dead moon on the live sea's breast,
Slain as with bitter fear to see the sun:
And eastward was a strong bright wind begun
Between the clouds and waters: and he said,
Seeing hardly through dark dawn her doubtful head;
"Iseult?" and like a death-bell faint and clear
The virgin voice rang answer—"I am here."
And his heart sprang, and sank again: and she
Spake, saying, "What would my knightly lord with me?"
And Tristram: "Hath my lady watched all night
Beside me, and I knew not? God requite
Her love for comfort shown a man nigh dead."

"Yea, God shall surely guerdon it," she said,
"Who hath kept me all my days through to this hour."

And Tristram: "God alone hath grace and power
To pay such grace toward one unworthier shown
Than ever durst, save only of God alone,
Crave pardon yet and comfort, as I would
Crave now for charity if my heart were good,
But as a coward's it fails me, even for shame."

Then seemed her face a pale funereal flame
That burns down slow by midnight, as she said:
"Speak, and albeit thy bidding spake me dead,
God's love renounce me if it were not done."

And Tristram: "When the sea-line takes the sun
That now should be not far off sight from far,

Look if there come not with the morning star
My ship bound hither from the northward back,
And if the sail be white thereof or black."

And knowing the soothfast sense of his desire
So sore the heart within her raged like fire
She could not wring forth of her lips a word,
But bowing made sign how humbly had she heard.
And the sign given made light his heart; and she
Set her face hard against the yearning sea
Now all athirst with trembling trust of hope
To see the sudden gates of sunrise ope;
But thirstier yearned the heart whose fiery gate
Lay wide that vengeance might come in to hate.
And Tristram lay at thankful rest, and thought
Now surely life nor death could grieve him aught,
Since past was now life's anguish as a breath,
And surely past the bitterness of death.
For seeing he had found at these her hands this grace,
It could not be but yet some breathing-space
Might leave him life to look again on love's own face.
"Since if for death's sake," in his heart he said,
"Even she take pity upon me quick or dead,
How shall not even from God's hand be compassion shed?
For night bears dawn, how weak soe'er and wan,
And sweet ere death, men fable, sings the swan.
So seems the Swan my signal from the sea
To sound a song that sweetens death to me
Clasped round about with radiance from above
Of dawn, and closer clasped on earth by love.
Shall all things brighten, and this my sign be dark?"

And high from heaven suddenly rang the lark,
Triumphant; and the far first refluent ray
Filled all the hollow darkness full with day.
And on the deep sky's verge a fluctuant light
Gleamed, grew, shone, strengthened into perfect sight,
As bowed and dipped and rose again the sail's clear white.
And swift and steadfast as a sea-mew's wing
It neared before the wind, as fain to bring
Comfort, and shorten yet its narrowing track.
And she that saw looked hardly toward him back,
Saying, "Ah, the ship comes surely; but her sail is black."
And fain he would have sprung upright, and seen,
And spoken: but strong death struck sheer between,
And darkness closed as iron round his head:
And smitten through the heart lay Tristram dead.

And scarce the word had flown abroad, and wail
Risen, ere to shoreward came the snowbright sail,
And lightly forth leapt Ganhardine on land,
And led from ship with swift and reverent hand
Iseult: and round them up from all the crowd
Broke the great wail for Tristram out aloud.
And ere her ear might hear her heart had heard,
Nor sought she sign for witness of the word;
But came and stood above him newly dead,
And felt his death upon her: and her head
Bowed, as to reach the spring that slakes all drouth;
And their four lips became one silent mouth.

So came their hour on them that were in life
Tristram and Iseult: so from love and strife
The stroke of love's own hand felt last and best
Gave them deliverance to perpetual rest.
So, crownless of the wreaths that life had wound,
They slept, with flower of tenderer comfort crowned;
From bondage and the fear of time set free,
And all the yoke of space on earth and sea
Cast as a curb for ever: nor might now
Fear and desire bid soar their souls or bow,
Lift up their hearts or break them: doubt nor grief
More now might move them, dread nor disbelief
Touch them with shadowy cold or fiery sting,
Nor sleepless languor with its weary wing,
Nor harsh estrangement, born of time's vain breath,
Nor change, a darkness deeper far than death.
And round the sleep that fell around them then
Earth lies not wrapped, nor records wrought of men
Rise up for timeless token: but their sleep
Hath round it like a raiment all the deep;
No change or gleam or gloom of sun and rain,
But all time long the might of all the main
Spread round them as round earth soft heaven is spread,
And peace more strong than death round all the dead.
For death is of an hour, and after death
Peace: nor for aught that fear or fancy saith,
Nor even for very love's own sake, shall strife
Perplex again that perfect peace with life.
And if, as men that mourn may deem or dream,
Rest haply here than there might sweeter seem.
And sleep, that lays one hand on all, more good
By some sweet grave's grace given of wold or wood
Or clear high glen or sunbright wind-worn down
Than where life thunders through the trampling town
With daylong feet and nightlong overhead,

What grave may cast such grace round any dead,
What so sublime sweet sepulchre may be
For all that life leaves mortal, as the sea?
And these, rapt forth perforce from earthly ground,
These twain the deep sea guards, and girdles round
Their sleep more deep than any sea's gulf lies,
Though changeless with the change in shifting skies,
Nor mutable with seasons: for the grave
That held them once, being weaker than a wave,
The waves long since have buried: though their tomb
Was royal that by ruth's relenting doom
Men gave them in Tintagel: for the word
Took wing which thrilled all piteous hearts that heard
The word wherethrough their lifelong lot stood shown,
And when the long sealed springs of fate were known,
The blind bright innocence of lips that quaffed
Love, and the marvel of the mastering draught,
And all the fraughtage of the fateful bark,
Loud like a child upon them wept King Mark,
Seeing round the sword's hilt which long since had fought
For Cornwall's love a scroll of writing wrought,
A scripture writ of Tristram's hand, wherein
Lay bare the sinless source of all their sin,
No choice of will, but chance and sorcerous art,
With prayer of him for pardon: and his heart
Was molten in him, wailing as he kissed
Each with the kiss of kinship—"Had I wist,
Ye had never sinned nor died thus, nor had I
Borne in this doom that bade you sin and die
So sore a part of sorrow." And the king
Built for their tomb a chapel bright like spring
With flower-soft wealth of branching tracery made
Fair as the frondage each fleet year sees fade,
That should not fall till many a year were done.
There slept they wedded under moon and sun
And change of stars: and through the casements came
Midnight and noon girt round with shadow and flame
To illume their grave or veil it; till at last
On these things too was doom as darkness cast:
For the strong sea hath swallowed wall and tower,
And where their limbs were laid in woful hour
For many a fathom gleams and moves and moans
The tide that sweeps above their coffined bones
In the wrecked chancel by the shivered shrine:
Nor where they sleep shall moon or sunlight shine
Nor man look down for ever: none shall say,
Here once, or here, Tristram and Iseult lay:
But peace they have that none may gain who live.

And rest about them that no love can give,
And over them, while death and life shall be,
The light and sound and darkness of the sea.

www.ingramcontent.com/pod-product-compliance
Lightning Source LLC
Chambersburg PA
CBHW060131050426

42448CB00010B/2061